TRANSFORMATIONAL
WRITING

*How to Manifest Your Desires
with Just Pen and Paper*

CELANDINE SADIE

Table of Contents

INTRODUCTION

*"You can always edit a bad page.
You can't edit a blank page." — Jodi Picoult*

Throughout our lives, we've been taught that success is achievable if you work hard. Put in the effort, and you will eventually reap the rewards. It's a concept that has been passed down from generation to generation, and it's been instilled so deeply in our DNA that thinking otherwise would be deemed ludicrous. Of course, things change, and as the world is dynamic, so too should our views be on how the world works.

There have been new ways of thinking that aim at achieving success through manifestation and visualizing your goals. Manifesting your goals will allow you a chance at infinite possibilities, will motivate you to work even harder at achieving them, and will bring you absolute joy and bliss as you take charge of your life. This is where the Law of Attraction comes in.

You might have heard of this theory once or twice through an array of self-help books, documentaries, or even celebrities and public figures endorsing the powers of the Law of Attraction. You might also have given it a go yourself but haven't yet seen any results. The Law of Attraction is a science that might seem tricky at first to understand and apply, and when you don't notice any desired results, you're bound to end up discouraged. Don't give up just yet! Once you get the hang of manifesting your goals and desires correctly, you'll find that it becomes a habit or a second nature to your thought process. That's why it's definitely worth knowing everything about the Law of Attraction as well as how to manifest your desires.

One way of doing this is through Transformational Writing. Using a pen and paper to truly achieve success and implement change within your life and personality is key in making your dreams and desires become a reality. Transformation is a multi-layered process; the first layer is to transform your thoughts and wishes into an art by writing them down. This book will take you through how you can manifest your goals by writing all your heart's desires using journaling, for example, and other transformative writing techniques. In the same way that carbon is transformed eventually into shiny diamonds, you can utilize your life's mission to transform your life into something magical. When we inspect our lives and goals and emit them into this art, we are then transformed as the writer of our own path.

According to Newberg & Waldmen, language affects and tailors our behavior. If we speak the right words in the right way, we can find our lives filled with love, money and all we desire. Spoken in the wrong way, though, words can lead to disasters. Everything we say is layered with personal meaning, and to truly achieve our goals, we need to carefully orchestrate what we say. (Newberg & Waldmen, 2012) Using meaningful words, whether written or spoken, will affect how you envision your life. When you say or write down phrases that start with "I should," or "I could," or even, "It's too hard to do," it can hinder your progress. Meanwhile, changing your terms to, "It's challenging, but I can do it," or, "I want, I will, I have decided," are definitely empowering and transformational.

This book aims at helping you through the thought processes needed to manifest your goals in the right way, to guide you through transformational writing techniques to make it a habit of manifesting your desires, as well as to understand what it means to visualize your aspirations and how to do it. When you learn the ins and outs of these techniques, you'll find that you're able to envision a much more successful future for yourself, one that is truly enriching.

But First, What is the Law of Attraction?

"We do not need magic to transform our world. We carry all of the power we need inside ourselves already."
— J.K. Rowling

Whether you're looking to make a current change or an impact in your life, or if you're simply looking to empower yourself for a wonderful future, you need to fully understand what the Law of Attraction is and how it works in your life. Everything can be achieved if you put your mind to it. Literally.

To put it simply, the Law of Attraction means you are able to attract whatever you need into your life. Let's say you want to get a certain job opportunity. The more you truly focus all your positive energy on it, the more likely you are to get it.

Ask for What You Want, Not What You Don't Want

"You get to choose what you want but you must get clear about what you want. This is your work."
— *Rhonda Byrne*

No matter what race or religion we belong to, we are all governed by the universe. When we send positive vibes out into the world, we will get rewarded from the universe as it is simply responding to our positive energy. Negative energy works in pretty much the same way; have you ever noticed that the more you're anxious, cynical, resentful, or angry, the more these factors you're worried about have a habit of always happening? Energy is a fickle concept that we all need to use to our advantage. Whatever energy you send out to the world, you'll always find it reciprocated.

You need to be clear about what you truly want, control your emotions, and believe that one day you will achieve it. And it can be applied to ANYTHING. For good measure, let's say you wish to do any of the following:

- You're about to embark on a new career path and arc looking to leave your old job behind.

- You're toying with the idea of moving to another country or state.

- You wish to become more secure, confident, and charismatic.

- You would like to earn more money and achieve greater success.

- You simply want a successful and meaningful relationship to last.

- You're just looking to adjust your mental state and well-being.

Whatever it is you're aiming for, you can use the powers of the Law of Attraction as well as manifesting your desires through transformational writing to take charge of your life.

The Law of Attraction in Ancient Teachings and History

Although the Law of Attraction is considered to be a "new" thought process, it actually has a significant mark in history, and many historical figures have used it to inspire change among the masses. For hundreds of years, it's been believed that this thought process originated from a range of ancient practices, especially ones created by Buddha. For decades, his teachings were to inspire many individuals and guide them on their journeys. He believed that all that we are is a result of what we have thought. Gandhi also advocated for a similar theory; he will forever remain in history as a social activist who led a successful civil rights movement for India against British rule. However, his teachings, to this day, inspire other civil rights movements across the globe as well as inner change among individuals. He also believed that a man is but the product of his thought. What he thinks, he becomes.

With the turn of the 19th century, it was also a time that catapulted New Thought into our traditions. Many writers and authors played key roles in the development of the Law of Attraction, even before this term was coined, as well as decades before modern books were inspired by them, like "The Secret." Some of the inspiration was drawn from "The Secret Doctrine" by the spiritual writer Helena Blavatsky. She believed that we were able to shape our realities just with the power of our thoughts, telling us not to fear our difficulties or wish for different circumstances. She believed that if we make the best of our problems, they become a stepping stone to opportunity.

As the 20th century rolled in, authors such as William Walker Atkinson were considered Law of Attraction practitioners who have led this new thought process to what we know today. He's written more than 100 books encouraging individuals to focus on their willpower, as well as how to truly manifest their desires to bring about good things in their lives. He's always encouraged others to "visualize your power" as well as "*to always try to improve yourself no matter where you are or what your position is. Learn all you can. Don't see how little you can do, but how much you can do.*"

By the mid-20th century, New Thought authors like Louise Hay were the key developers in the power of affirmations to support your goals. Other authors like W. Clement Stone and Napoleon Hill have co-authored books encouraging people to attract success into their lives. They both believed that "*whatever the mind of man can conceive and believe, it can achieve.*"

Celebrities and Public Figures Who Endorse Law of Attraction

In the 21st century, "The Secret" by Rhonda Byrne was an instant success; it has turned the ancient teachings and beliefs of the Law of Attraction from a new age niche to a globally accepted concept with over 20 million copies sold worldwide. Byrne believed that we need to be truly awake to receive answers from a universe that has already been answering us all our lives. (Byrne, 2006) The documentary of the same name was able to further push what Law of Attraction practitioners believed, as well as including inspirational success stories from common individuals. It contains insights and teachings from practitioners that empower the manifestation approach, making it a huge success. This has also led to an influx of celebrities who were influenced by it.

Many celebrities and public figures have endorsed the powers of the Law of Attraction and aimed to prove how it has changed their lives. Oprah, for example, celebrates this new thought process and claims it's one of the ways that has shaped her life completely. Needless to say, she's a world-renowned talk show host, actress, and philanthropist. She also leads a business empire that can inspire any business owner. She believes that the more you celebrate your life and praise it, the more you will receive and have to celebrate; *"The way you think creates reality for yourself."*

The world-renowned author, public speaker, and a prominent figure in the New Age Movement, Deepak Chopra, is a firm believer in the powers of the Law of Attraction, only if used right. He believes that the Law of Attraction isn't just about wishing your desires without expecting obstacles, because these roadblocks will eventually lead to your goals. When you reflect on who you really are and what you want, you'll be able to tackle these obstacles; *"Once you see it is only you reflecting yourself back, what happens? You become more self-aware. As self-awareness expands, you become much clearer and focused on what you truly want. Then and only then can the law of attraction work for you reliably."* (Chopra, 2019)

Actors like Will Smith and Jim Carrey have given interviews on many occasions praising the benefits they've reaped from applying the Law of Attraction to their lives. Smith advocates the need to believe in yourself and go for whatever you believe in to achieve it; *"Our thoughts, our feelings, our dreams, our ideas are physical in the universe.*" He accredits his massive success in Hollywood to how he's applied the Law of Attraction, and he recommends that his greatness is applicable to anyone.

Likewise, Carrey acknowledges how applying the Law of Attraction has helped him become a millionaire. When he was first starting out, he didn't have a single dollar to his name. And so, he resorted to visualizing techniques by creating a dream check, which eventually resulted in his paycheck of $10 million dollars when he achieved success in the film industry. He once said in an interview with Oprah, "It's just about letting the universe know what you want and then working towards it while letting go of how it comes to pass." Arnold Schwarzenegger, another believer of the Law of Attraction, didn't only witness his success in the film industry but also in the political world as the Governor of California from 2003 to 2011. He claimed that he'd been using visualizing techniques early in his career, as early as his bodybuilding days and winning Mr. Universe; "I visualized myself being a famous actor and earning big money. I could feel and taste success. I just knew it would all happen."

Musicians are familiar with the concept of the Law of Attraction as well. The rapper and business mogul Jay-Z, as well as superstar, Oscar-winner, actress, and singer Lady Gaga have both claimed that the Law of Attraction is the reason why they're so successful. When asked how he's become so lucky, Jay-Z believes that only you can create your own luck. If you believe in yourself and your talent, you can achieve what you want. Meanwhile, Lady Gaga has always spoken about the power of affirmations by saying if you repeat it to yourself every day, envisioning success will eventually lead to it. Needless to say, her recent stint in "A Star is Born" has earned her an Oscar and a Grammy award. These success stories are enough to show you how the Law of Attraction works and should surely inspire you to start applying it.

The Law of Attraction in Today's World

The more we discover about the effects of the Law of Attraction, the less skeptical people become. It is difficult for many people in this age of advanced science and technology to believe that all they have to do is merely 'think' something and that it will come true. This, in fact, is not all it takes to apply the Law of Attraction. It is also the reason why so many people that have experienced it firsthand have taken to educating others as much as they can, using statistics and step by step methodology to enlighten them.

Psychology plays a huge role in the Law of Attraction. There is a lot of work to be done on a mental level in order for this to work. You'll find references to people from all walks of life who will be able to paint a better picture as to why the Law of Attraction has been around for so long, and how it works. The fact of the matter is - and anyone who's successfully living with it will agree - it takes a considerable amount of work. If the effort isn't put in, then, of course, nothing will happen! Later on, in the book, we give you examples of influential people who have worked hard in their lives and have been able to reach many people by sharing their experiences with the Law of Attraction. Victoria Gallagher, who was initially a professional hypnotherapist, now educates people in a way that helps them discover what they need to do in order to make the Law of Attraction work for them, the way it did for her with the help of hypnotherapy and her discoveries about the subconscious mind. Along with Victoria, there are people like Louise Hay, who overcame cancer using the power of the Law of Attraction and became a success in her life, and now, she too, gives seminars, talks, and tutorials on how to make it work, reaching hundreds, if not thousands of people from all over the world.

You can find statements from people from all walks of life that have tried and now live by the Law of Attraction, simply because they learned the correct way of implementing it; which is what this book will be able to do in great detail.

Overview

To give you an idea of what the entire book will cover, it's important for you to know what you will be learning and discovering about yourself in order to reach that higher understanding of yourself as well as your perception of the world around you. These are the two key factors required in order to achieve success in applying the Law of Attraction. We will begin with going over the science behind the Law of Attraction and then move toward understanding the importance of accessing the different levels of consciousness in order to actually have the Law of Attraction work consistently with you. The secret behind that is learning how to get through each of the steps in detail, what they mean and why they can work for you.

Once you have understood the meaning and purpose of the Law of Attraction, you can then move on to putting it to practice. By learning the importance of the role of writing within the Law of Attraction, you will be able to discover an amazing tool that will not only help you understand your desires and needs, but will also give you the consistency that you need. The whole point of the Law of Attraction is to be able to have the correct outlook on life in order to achieve your dreams and goals. To do so successfully, you will learn *how* to write and how to edit your writing effectively so that you can finally have the Law of Attraction as a way of life for you.

Who is this book for?

There is not a single person on this planet that cannot use the power of the Law of Attraction to their benefit. The beauty of this book is that it covers all grounds needed to help you understand what the Law of Attraction is, how you can relate to it, and how to use it in everyday life.

We all have dreams, desires, and goals that we think of on a daily basis. We all often wonder why we cannot reach out and make these dreams come true, and we think that these things are unattainable. This book guides you through the journey of self-discovery so that you are able to alter your perception, understand the concept of energy, and the steps you need to take and implement into your daily routine and thought process to be able to achieve your goals in the most natural way imaginable. You will finally gain an understanding of *why* intent, energy, and the concept of vibrations are vital to your growth. What is special about this book is that you will learn how to utilize different methods of writing as the main tool for keeping you on top of your game and to guide you in using the Law of Attraction to achieve your goals through Transformational Writing.

The Process

It's important that you are aware of what the process will be like as you move through your journey of life while using the Law of Attraction. There won't be magic, and nothing will appear out of thin air as you sit back and dream of it! The Law of Attraction is first and foremost, a *process*; one that involves hard work, but you will be more than willing to put the time in because all of it is fruitful, every step of the way.

You're going to learn about how to perceive the world, the people around you and yourself differently. You are also going to delve deep into your past, and you're going to have to do a lot of soul searching and self-analysis so that you can understand and alter the roots of your insecurities - those that which have been holding you back from living the best way you can.

There are going to be different methods of self-discovery, and ups and downs, but the best part is that you are going to become *creative.* You are going to learn how to write and express everything you know, and even things you didn't think you knew about yourself and the way you see the world. By using this writing with the skills we'll provide, you will be able to transform your thought process by accessing your subconscious mind and making changes to the way you think and live. Ultimately, you will have a better understanding of who you are, why you are the way you are, and what it is you need to succeed. You will probably find a few surprises along the way, because the truth is, we are on an endless journey of self-discovery, as we are growing and changing with the experiences we have every day. The process of your journey with the Law of Attraction through Transformational Writing is one that is bound to change your life, certainly for the better.

ABOUT THE AUTHOR

Celandine Sadie is a life coach who specializes in the Law of Attraction and creative writing. She believes that writing is a powerful tool to channel our feelings and desires. She studied art therapy and later on became a certified Mindfulness teacher. After several years of one-on-one coaching, she decided to publish her knowledge in a book and share her wisdom with a bigger audience.

Celandine has spent several years in Bali and India, where she went through a transformational spiritual journey. She teaches creative writing from the depths of her heart and has an empathetic approach toward her clients. Celandine allows her clients to open up in a safe space where she encourages vulnerability.

SECTION 1

UNDERSTANDING AND ACHIEVING THE SKILL TO MANIFEST YOUR DESIRES

As A Token
of My Gratitude...

Here is a **FREE** video training course on how to develop
Relentless Optimism

Positive thinking is a state of mind that naturally expects a
positive outcome to events. Not all of us were born to be
positive thinkers. The good news is that this mindset is a
habit that can be developed and enhanced.

The benefits are greater happiness and the increased likelihood that you will be able to achieve whatever goals you create for yourself. Positive thinking knows no limits, while negative thoughts only create limitations.

Click the picture of the DVD box or navigate to the link below to claim your copy now!

https://tinyurl.com/RelentlessOptimism

CHAPTER 1

The Science Behind Law of Attraction

"The more willing you are to surrender to the energy within you, the more power can flow through you."
-- Shakti Gawain

Over the years, quite a few misconceptions about the Law of Attraction have risen; it has often been criticized as a theory that lacks substance or as being another hippie excuse for bad luck. While there isn't a decisive scientific model for the Law of Attraction, there have been commonly accepted scientific principles, theories, studies, and research that supports the existence and the efficacy of it. To put it plainly, the Law of Attraction means when you send out positive vibrations to the universe to 'attract' something you desire. By manifesting your goals, thoughts, and wishes, you're aiming to direct all your energy at achieving whatever success you wish to have, and you will eventually reap the rewards. In truth, it's more than just a concept or theory, it's a way of life, and if implemented right, it can be life-changing. A large number of people have attested to its effectiveness and have shared their inspiring success stories to the world. And, like all good theories, it is backed by science to support it.

Research in psychology and neuroscience has explored the effect of the Law of Attraction on an individual's life. One very significant study was conducted to prove the power of positive thinking and its strong connection to our overall satisfaction and contentment in life. Korean researchers published this study in Yonsei Medical Journal after conducting it on 400 participants. They've claimed that there is a relationship between positive thinking and life satisfaction, based on their results, and that thinking positively ultimately increases the satisfaction we feel towards the world. (Yonsei Medical Journal, 2007)

Positive thinking not only restores life satisfaction, but it also benefits your health greatly. It has been proven that optimistic thinking boosts your self-confidence, your immunity, as well as making you more resilient to roadblocks and stress. This alone helps adjust your blood pressure levels. And it can only mean that the way we approach life by using positive thoughts, goal manifestation, and the Law of Attraction, the healthier we become physically and mentally. When you lead a content life, you're more motivated and engaged to pursue what you thought you never would, thus leading to the success you've so desired.

Psychologists and neurologists have both aimed to prove the effect the Law of Attraction has on our brains and psyches. Several scientists believe that visualization creates a better future because you're constructing your brain. In a study entitled "The Construction of the Brain," scientists believed that constructing a hypothetical situation in your imagination is crucial to planning for the future and that imagining new experiences is construction in its purest form. (Hassabis & Maguire, 2009) Meanwhile, psychologists have claimed that affirmations are powerful enough to reduce anxiety and depression, recover from trauma, and improve anticipatory planning.

However, with all the theories, studies, and research, the Law of Attraction can be summarized in one word: Energy.

Everything is Energy: The Power of Your Thought Vibrations

"The vibrations of mental forces are the finest and consequently the most powerful in existence"
- Charles Haanel

When two people are in love, they become in sync with their movements and their thoughts, and it almost seems effortless, like they're slow-dancing on melted caramel. The fact that everything works together and flows well refers to their energy, it's also the reason for their mutual attraction. This attraction is one of the most profound energies that can be utilized not only in relationships but in any aspect of your life.

Since the dawn of time, many spiritual teachings have believed that the universe is part of an interconnected web of energy. Science has also proved that everything around us is energy through physics. Ever since the 1900s, New Science has advocated how the universe is made up of a flow of energies, and not matter. As humans, our five senses can sense and release a multitude of energy through vibrations; we might not feel it, but it ends up connecting to everything we experience. We have the free will and ability to control our thoughts in a way that we can control our own energy and direct it sensibly.

Our thoughts are vibrations, and the energy they will seek out will most certainly match; the Law of Attraction means that energy attracts itself to other energy it identifies with. It differentiates between what we see with our naked eye and what we can tangibly control, to what we cannot see or touch, like radio waves. Everything comes in waves: storms, the ocean, or thunder, and they all resemble a wave of emotion, don't they? Your brain is actually the most powerful electromagnetic processing tool; when you learn how to utilize the energy you release or are subjected to, you'll be able to send out the right thought waves to the universe. The power of thoughts, their waves, and vibrations, isn't something trivial or something that should be underestimated.

Unfortunately, many people become trapped in never-ending negative energy and they wonder why their life isn't going the way they want it to. When you focus all your energy on negative thoughts, you'll find that what resonates are negative life elements. The more you focus on what bothers you, the more it always has a habit of sticking around. It's the same concept with focusing on positive energy; when you focus all your energy on bliss and abundance, then bliss and abundance are what you will find. Consider wealthy people who become wealthier - they know how to channel their energy to bring them imminent success. They believe that they can shape their own reality according to what they desire the most. Another example is if you are about to be interviewed for a job you wish to have, you should attend that interview believing that, without a shadow of a doubt, you will get offered the position you're after.

"Your positive thought energy will, through the level of the human mind, influence the mind of the interviewer in your favor. This is why many successful business people almost always succeed in consistently winning large business deals; they always know even before they enter into the initial negotiations that they will certainly win the deal without question. The thought of not winning such a deal never even once enters their mind, they simply know it as a foregone conclusion." (Cooper, 2007)

❖ The way you control your thoughts doesn't mean you only focus all your energy onto a certain circumstance or a life choice. On the contrary, it means that you need to turn it into a mindset, a habit, or a way of life

Rewiring Your Brain: How your Reticular Activating System (RAS) can be trained to see the positive

When you look back at conversations with friends or family, you will notice that there's a thought pattern that constantly brings negativity. They will probably be thinking:

- How they can't pay off their debts, and they're always broke.

- How they will never get the job they really wanted because they're not skilled enough.

- How they're not confident enough to start a new relationship.

- How they will never be able to quit the job they loathe and start their business because they're not brave enough.

- How they will never lose weight because their body isn't responding to their weight-loss program.

You might have been guilty yourself if any of these aforementioned thoughts crossed your mind, and you notice that you have trapped yourself into a prison-cell of your own creation. It's easy to only focus on the negative aspects of your life. You're always subjected to factors that will bring you down, whether it comes from people telling you can't do whatever it is you desire, or you bring yourself down due to insecurity issues and a lack of belief in your abilities. Our society is programmed to see the missing holes within it instead of the complete picture.

The media, as an example, is one element that always reminds you that you need more without providing a way on how to achieve it. Instead, you end up comparing your failures to other people's successes, which isn't a fair comparison, to say the least. The media also constantly displays the negatives in the world in order to bring awareness to an issue, but not all of it is to spark change. When you understand the purpose of it all, it makes you wonder why you're even listening to these negative thoughts. If you have a background in marketing, you'll know that the reason for this is just to raise viewership and ratings. When negative topics are aired constantly on your TV or any media outlet, you'll be hooked. On the other hand, it doesn't work the same with positive topics. Marketing has taken utter advantage of human psychology, and when you understand this method, you can easily distance yourself and not be impacted by negativity.

Easier said than done, right? Not entirely. One thing you need to understand is that these negative thoughts or biases were hardwired into the brain since the dawn of time. During prehistoric times or the age of 'cavemen,' the brain was always primed to allude and focus on the negative as a way to survive. Man needed to make sure that he is safe, well-fed, and surrounded by allies. When focusing on the negative, it allowed him to fight for survival. However, time has evolved drastically, and so should your brain.

The brain is a complex device that is not fully utilized yet. But it does have the power to sort through billions of data at any time without malfunctioning. It actually has the power to organize every bit of data you're subjected to. This is where the Reticular Activating System (RAS) comes into play. Your RAS is a bundle of nerves located at the brain stem and filters through copious amounts of data and, according to what you focus on, it will only present you with what is vital and important. RAS is how you can tune yourself out of a crowded place with noise and people talking, but can pay attention if someone called your name or something that sounds like it. It's also when you recently purchased a certain item, like a car, and you start seeing it everywhere you go. Your RAS has distinguished that this is something valuable and frequently allows you to recognize it.

The beauty of RAS is that it is self-programmed to work in your favor without you actively doing anything. Similarly, it can seek information that fuels the validation of your beliefs; RAS helps you see what you want to see, thus influencing your actions. It has the ability to filter the world you're living through the limitations you create and, by doing so, your beliefs actually shape these boundaries. If you believe you can't achieve a certain task, even if it's as simple as weight-loss, you'll end up sending signals to your brain telling yourself that you really can't lose weight, and you won't.

This way, you'll come to understand that the Law of Attraction isn't so mysterious or far-fetched. When you focus on unfavorable aspects in your life, you'll end up inviting negativity only into your world. However, when you focus on desirable outcomes and positive elements, you'll end up shaping your reality to become more optimistic and satisfactory as these positive elements will continuously exist in your world. Because of your RAS, your brain will actively seek positivity out and will influence your actions.

Training your RAS to translate your subconscious to the conscious might seem a little tricky, but with practice, it will become second nature to you. It's all about setting your intent, by focusing hard on your goals or dreams, your RAS will show you the necessary information or opportunities that will help you make these dreams a reality. When you truly visualize what you desire, you're allowing your subconscious and conscious to work together to achieve it. Even if you face obstacles along the way, they're all part of your journey, and so is failure. You need to be able to develop your mental muscles to expect failure and deal with its consequences without being disheartened. What is failure but an experience to learn, to transform, and to progress in life? Detach from discouraging and negative thoughts and focus all your energy on what you truly want to see filling up your life, by doing so, your RAS will show you these aspects and will prove to you that it can be done. Rewiring your brain will allow you to become more aware of your surroundings and your desires, thus sending out positive vibrations to the universe.

When you set your intent, you'll allow your RAS to reach toward your desired goals and will allow you to enjoy your future journey getting there. You can apply this method established by a research article entitled "Neuroscience & Creating an Optimal Future for Yourself."

First, think of the goal you want to set your intent for or the situation you want to achieve. Next, set an intention for yourself in regards to what experience you are looking to have in that situation. This is an important step. Now, in the case that other people may be involved, what is the kind of interaction you would like to have with them? Set that as an intent. Interactions can vary between having fun, being productive, or learning something new. And finally, create a sort of mental movie of that perfect, future situation. Take note of everything you are experiencing in the situation. What are you seeing? What are you feeling? Are you talking, or saying things to yourself? (Hallbom & Hallbom)

Another method you can apply is by using your own writing to transform how your RAC operates. Consider this daily writing exercise:

- For 5-10 minutes each day set a timer, and write in a journal everything you've achieved. It can be anything from graduating, to getting a new job, and to marrying the love of your life. Keep writing until you run out of ideas to put down on paper.

- The timer will still be ticking, so mention minor things you've achieved like organizing the chaos in your closet or finally finishing the book you've wanted to read.

- The idea here is that you're training your brain only to see the achievements, and by doing so, your brain will automatically and continuously look for what is great in your life. This is when you focus on other future achievements you would like to see happening in your life. And by doing so, your brain will be rewired to motivate you towards your goals.

Law of Attraction in the World of Science

Many of us are willing to try new methods by which we can materialize our desires and are more open to different approaches and theories, but there are just as many people out there who need more than just theories. Even though many academics in the world of science may identify it under the umbrella of pseudoscience, the theories are very much applicable to real-life experimentation, and the results are credible. The wonderful thing about the Law of Attraction is that the concept has been around long enough for people within the academic world to take note and go forward in conducting research to delve deeper into the way it works and the effect it has on different people.

❖ **Victoria M. Gallagher:**
   A Pioneer Worth Mentioning

If there's an academic worth mentioning when it comes to the implementation of the Law of Attraction in real-life situations, and really going into the details of it all, then it is Victoria M. Gallagher. Originally a seasoned hypnotherapist, she was already knee-deep in treating psychological ailments through alternatives to medicine.

Hypnotherapy comes from the same school of thought as LOA as the treatment aims to treat stress and even trauma without the use of any external factors, primarily medication. It allows both the hypnotist, as well as the patient, to look into areas of the mind that have never been tapped into before in order to find the source of self-destructive or trauma-induced behavior.

Victoria was intuitive enough to link the fundamentals of the age-old practice of hypnotism to those of the theory of Law of Attraction, and stood to ensure that the word would get out to the masses in a way that was relatable and practical, and applicable to everyday life, even for the simplest of people, or the most skeptical. Law of Attraction is a concept that basically needs to be applied on a subconscious level, and hypnosis works to tap into the subconscious mind. This is how Victoria came to be a primary pioneer for LOA.

❖ **Shaun Gallagher:**
   Explains Mirror Neurons from another
   perspective

Mirror neurons, as defined in the way most scientists have found, are the neurons that fire up when we, as humans, identify behavior and copy it. These neurons exist in many animals, as well. They have been set for deep speculation as finding it as solely a physical function, and not one that is triggered by an aspect relative to our consciousness, and how the Law of Attraction in particular plays into its function is something that has been up for debate.

This is where Shaun Gallagher comes in. He brought to the world's attention that the mirror neuron is not merely a bodily response. He wrote a book titled 'How the Body Shapes the Mind' where he addressed the question and the relevance of how these functions are not merely mechanical but are responses and results of emotional effects. The Law of Attraction comes into play here in that body function is separate from the body image, and that ultimately, how we perceive our bodies to be affects their function. He clarifies the fact that mirror neurons allow us the capacity for one body to identify the other, whether it be in physical appearance or in identifying energies. We don't go around copying every single thing we see every stranger doing.

He gives a great example of how, if someone pushes you, your body has no choice but to react by either falling or cushioning the fall somehow - it's a reflex reaction that you don't really have time to think of as such. But with other reactions, such as that which is related to mirror neurons, your subconscious is actively analyzing and helping in making the final decision of mirroring an action or behavior.

He put it perfectly himself in clarifying how pure science combined together with neuroscience and the quest to understand spirituality can lead people to better understand how the Law of Attraction plays into understanding the mind and body connect. According to him, we don't need concepts like 'universal spirituality' to help explain how intersubjective relations work, but we can rely on the neuroscience of inter-corporeality. (Gallagher, 2006).

❖ **Masaru Emoto:**
   Water Experiment & Consciousness

Masaru Emoto caused quite a ruckus in the scientific pool of researchers because of his controversial claims after conducting the notoriously well-known "Water Experiment." While ruffling a few feathers, his experiment did hold quite a bit of value in terms of explaining human consciousness and its effectiveness.

Emoto's experiment was basically about collecting water samples and exposing them to different kinds of vibrations and energies in the form of different kinds of music and words and images. He would then proceed to freeze the water and magnify it to photograph the results at a microscopic level and compare notes. He claimed that negative or dark triggers would result in less pleasing angles to the crystallization, while positive would produce more aesthetically appealing crystallization. He went a step further to prove his point by displaying the crystallization of water from a healthy and serene source, as opposed to that from a polluted source. But to no avail within the scientific community.

However, we must always remember that most breakthrough discoveries in any genre come from people who are initially thought to be crazy or delving into an area that most people think is impossible or non-existent. While the naysayers are losing their heads by defying and denying experimentation and discoveries in relation to energy and vibrations, these scientists are actually giving us knowledge that we can only see if we stop to think for a moment of what really was in play.

When an infant comes into this world, they are made up of up to 78% water, and this eventually reduces to up to 65%. Water is a very prevalent and important part of our composition. And what Emoto has proven to us is that, whether from within you or from your surrounding environment, be it physical or unconscious, energy and vibrations do affect us in a big way. The Law of

Attraction is evident and brought to light in Emoto's experiment in more than one way, and it proves to show how external factors play into our overall physical composition, which will inevitably affect us mentally as well.

❖ **Empirical Studies & First Hand Experiences That Support Law of Attraction**

Empirical studies are experiments and research that is conducted based purely on observation. These are great as a reference because they give an insight into how others have been able to use the Law of Attraction and have actually seen results. These kinds of studies provide proper records of their experiences.

❖ **Dr. John Wheeler:**
The Fundamental Connection Between the Universe & Consciousness

Dr. John Wheeler is one of the biggest names in the world of Physics as he coined popular terms such as 'Black Hole' and 'Wormhole.' He was also responsible for explaining to the world what nuclear fission is all about and a number of other theories in physics, as well as working with the amazing Albert Einstein.

Wheeler contributed a wonderful gift to the development of the Law of Attraction by presenting to the world the observation that for the universe to even exist, something was required to observe it. Consciousness and the universe were fundamentally interrelated. You couldn't have one without the other. (Wheeler & Folger, 2002).

He conducted an experiment called the 'delayed-choice' experiment, where he took an age-old experiment called the 'double-slit' experiment and put his own spin on it. To explain it simply, it shows how, when the light that comes through the slits and hits a strip of photographic film, it's observed by photon detectors and record the results. With the photon detectors on, the results differ from when the detectors are off, which were shocking and unexpected results.

By providing this observation, Wheeler brought to the world the knowledge that in order for something to be existent to the mind, it has to observe and acknowledge it. He discovered that perception and observation of something in the present affect the form of its existence in the past.

Let's say that you had a difficult childhood. As a result, you're bound to always look at it in a dark and negative way, and you will definitely link many of your insecurities and bad choices to these experiences. But what do you think would happen if you changed your perception of the events of your childhood? If you look back and see them as life lessons that taught you about human behavior, and how to become a stronger and independent individual, your outlook on the world around you would change. You would credit the rough experiences to being the cause of your ability to be self-sufficient and more empathetic to those around you.

❖ **Louise Hay:**
  A Success Story through LOA

Louise Hay lived a life that was full of tribulations and struggles from the moment she was born. She had a difficult childhood, and, as a teenager, she suffered bouts of abuse until she could take no more and decided to run away. Things started to look up for her as she became a successful model, and ended up marrying a wealthy man. Her journey to finding the gift of the Law of Attraction only began after her marriage ended, and she sought to find a way to fill the void that she could still not fill, even though she had led a decent life as an adult. By attending church, seminars, and trying to find ways to find herself again, she became the go-to person for self-help guidance and healing, and she made a career out of it not long after.

While doing extensive research on mental and physical illnesses, she discovered a way to reverse many of the symptoms that aggravated most of the illnesses using the power of the mind. Louise found that by using self-affirmation, visualization, keeping a healthy diet and lifestyle, as well as seeking the support of a psychotherapist helped her to find herself and climb her way out of her own illness- she was diagnosed with cancer and was able to come out of it successfully using the methods of the Law of Attraction.

❖ **Ellen Langer:**
   Reversing Age

Ellen Langer is a professor of Psychology at Harvard University, and she brought to light a very interesting realization through a case study. She believed that being 'old' was a state of mind that was conditioned by society and that just because you were above a certain age, it did not mean that you have to conform to the expectations of being a 'senior citizen.'

So she conducted an experiment where she brought a number of people who were between 70 to 80 years of age and put them in an environment that was specifically tailored to make them feel like they were in a time where they were much younger. She asked one of the groups to sit and speak of the times when they were younger, in the '50s, while the other group were requested to *behave* as if they were actually living in the '50s when they were much younger.

What the results showed was, even though the group that spoke of their experiences did show improvements in their overall physical and mental well-being, the other group who acted and behaved as they did when they were younger showed even more improvement than the first group.

There were even comparisons of before and after photos of the subjects that acted that they were younger, and there were clearly evident changes in their appearances that made them look much younger after the experiment. (Grierson, 2014)

By conducting this experiment, Ellen has shown the world that the methods used in the Law of Attraction are truly effective. The power of the mind and the thoughts that we instill in it affects our behavior, and this creates a domino effect on everything within us and around us.

If we strive to control the thoughts in our minds and take action on the people and the surroundings we live in, this will do wonders for our wellbeing and allow us to fulfill our desires.

❖ Evidence to the validity of LOA is on the Rise

With the ever-impressive rise in technological advances, scientists are slowly but surely taking the reality of energy and vibrations into scientific consideration in a big way. The world of neurology has access to viewing brain activity in more accurate ways than ever before. Brain scans are able to show brain activity, reacting to meditation, music, emotions, and so on. These are all studies that are catching the attention of many scientists as it gives evidence that human energy and vibrations are not just ravings of what they once thought to be pseudoscientific experiments.

Scientists, as well as everyday people, have all been discovering the effectiveness and longevity of the Law of Attraction, and how much of an impact it has on their lives - their health, lifestyle, and their overall wellbeing take a turn that is hard to go back from.

Different Levels of Consciousness

In order to be able to really implement the Law of Attraction in a natural and effective way in your daily life, you must first understand the different levels of consciousness and become wholly aware of them within yourself and what they stand for.

We all have three levels of consciousness, and those are the Conscious, Subconscious, and finally, the Super Conscious state of being.

1. Conscious

The conscious state of mind is the one at the very surface and is generally problem-oriented. This means that this is where we tend to take everything we see and hear at face value and process it using our primary senses. This is where everything that we are consciously aware of and are therefore thinking of is at the forefront.

While we are able to function just fine with the awareness of our conscious level, it lacks the depth needed to actually make wholesome decisions. Doing so solely based on fact and not tapping into your emotions and thought process on a deeper level might prove to be problematic. The conscious mind, however, is not as shallow as it may seem. You need to be aware of what your process is consciously in order to be able to get to the next level of consciousness.

2. **Subconscious**

Some may argue that the subconscious level of being is the first, and not the conscious. This is because it is the state where our memories are stored and where our dreams are formed and met. Actions and thoughts that you probably have no recollection of are stored in this area and may come up in the form of what we like to call a 'Deja-vu' or simply, in our dreams.

It's important to know that the subconscious is not far off from our conscious actions and decisions. We may not be consciously aware of it, but the things stored within our subconscious play a large role in how we move forward in our thought process. Becoming more aware of our past and what stuck with us helps us to strengthen the way in which we make our decisions. This is because you learn to forge a better understanding of why you tend to shy away from certain situations and gravitate towards others. You are able to realign your ability to relate and understand how Law of Attraction works in regards to triggers.

3. **Super conscious**

The super conscious is super important because this is where it all comes together. Too many of us are so caught up in the material aspects of our lives that we are bound to overlook the things that make us who we are. The super conscious is where your intuition is free to work without restraint. Your raw emotions, the sources of your traumas and abilities that you have yet to tap into are hidden over here.

While this is a difficult level of consciousness to grasp entirely because of how heavy and complex it is, once you have understood how it works and how you can utilize it in a positive way, you'll find that this state of consciousness is where you'll be able to access all your truths, and once you master the art of accessing the super conscious state, it will no longer be a weight.

In order to utilize the Law of Attraction in all its glory, it's important for you to be able to be aware of the different levels of consciousness that make you, and those around you, who you really are. All these states are connected, and the more you become aware of how the mechanism of your mind works, the more enlightened you will become.

The Triangle of Cognitive Behavior

After understanding the purpose of each of your conscious states, the natural next step is knowing what tools you need to be able to identify what is going on within you. You will never be able to truly decipher what your intuition is telling you unless you are well versed in understanding what your thoughts, feelings, and actions arise from, how they affect one another, and what the results may be, and why, of course!

The Cognitive Triangle was coined in the field of cognitive-behavioral therapy in order to help people with mental disorders control their feelings by changing their cognitions and behaviors. This is an extremely helpful concept to take on as a person in general, not just for people who have emotional or mental disorders. To give more insight, these concepts can be broken down.

Thoughts

We have all, at one point or another, connected the fact that the things we think about affect the way we feel at any given time. It's important that we stay aware of this fact to the point where you are able to manage the way that you feel. When you are presented with a situation, you need to be actively aware of what it makes you think about. For instance, let's say that you are a person who once witnessed their mother being slapped on the face as a child. A friend of your strikes up a conversation and laughs about how they saw someone getting slapped and thought it was funny. The thoughts and images of your mother being slapped immediately come into play, and you begin to feel angry, upset, and anxious. These thoughts will tense you up, and you won't even understand the context that your friend is telling the story in, you'll only become resentful towards your friend, thinking that they are cold and heartless, and resort to responding in a defensive manner. Is there a way that you could have confronted these thoughts and managed your reaction differently?

It's important that we realize, first, that there are three different categories to our cognition:

1. **AUTOMATIC THOUGHTS:** These are the thoughts stored in our subconscious that we have no control over. They appear in your conscious mind when triggered by a word, an image, or even another basic thought. As mentioned in the example above,

these kinds of thoughts are the ones that need to be managed in order to move forward and really get a hold of applying the Law of Attraction to your thought process.

2. **SELF ENGAGEMENT:** In order to manage the automatic thoughts, the best way to do so is by talking yourself through it. Understand why the thought came up, why it made you feel the way you do, and what it is you could possibly do to alter your reaction. Understand that these thoughts are there, and take note of what the triggers are, and most importantly, remember that only you can overcome and control how deeply it affects you and whether you react positively or negatively. You must also talk yourself through the possible implications of the consequences- will your reaction hurt you or others?

3. **FUNDAMENTAL BELIEFS:** We all have core beliefs that exist within our minds from a very early age. We build upon them as we grow older, and we can alter them to better ourselves. Some fundamental beliefs are what give you strength in your foundation, and others actually contribute to tearing it down. So it is extremely important to reassess these thoughts. Understand that these beliefs are formed early on in

your life, and influence the way you perceive the world, the people in it, and most importantly, yourself. If any of these beliefs contribute to a negative view to any of these aspects, then this should raise a red flag and indicate that it's time to change it.

Behaviors

Just as your thoughts affect the way you feel, the way you behave affects your feelings as well. Yes, our actions are a manifestation of our feelings, but our behavior can alter these feelings as well. Many of us overlook this, and we get caught up in unhealthy cycles because we are simply unable to identify that sometimes, it is the behavior that takes a toll on the feelings.

The most common example of this is an unstable sleeping routine. It starts off as one night where you decide to stay out and party with your friends, which, of course, means that you're going to bed at around 3 a.m. You sleep in the next morning just because you can! Wake up at 1 in the afternoon, and this means you're able to stay up again, even for longer. Without even realizing, this becomes a routine and a habit, not because you can't control it but because it started off small and became a part of your daily routine. Soon, you end up sleeping less, or more than you should, and this, in turn, affects your demeanor.

You're never fresh, you don't have a clear head, you're always snapping at people, and you're just never in the mood for interaction.

The good news is that this can work on the other side of the spectrum as well. If you start doing something that makes you feel good once, think about doing it regularly, and you'll find that by doing this activity, you're in a better mood. You feel better about yourself, you treat the people around you with more calmness and consideration because you have something to look forward to in your day. To have something that you want to wake up for in the morning is really a concept that we overlook and take for granted. It doesn't have to be grand; it can be something as simple as going to the park every day to read a chapter from a book, or joining a group or a club that involves an interest that you have a liking for.

Being able to combine the efforts put forward towards thought, and understanding the process of behavior is a precious and effective tool. Becoming aware of how both affect your feelings allows you to have a stronger hold on all levels of your consciousness. This, in turn, allows you to strategically move forward in controlling your energy and the vibrations that you put out and attract, alike.

CHAPTER 2

Operating Principles for Consistently Getting Results

There is no greater sense of security and stability than by being able to have consistency. This is what makes the Law of Attraction so much more powerful than any other ideology. The Law of Attraction works on a different level than most because of the attention to detail and the ability to implement concepts into your life that are within your reach, while being intrinsically life-changing. It provides you with tools to think, adjust and create in ways that can last throughout the journey of your lifetime, and it is a wonderful work in progress that allows you to discover yourself while giving substance to those around you as well.

In order to truly understand how and why the Law of Attraction is a consistently rewarding approach, it's important to go into the operating principles and understand what they are all about.

GIVE LIFE TO SUBCONSCIOUS THOUGHTS

We have so many thoughts throughout the day that they can only be described as fleeting. We barely act upon a fraction of them, and they're usually the ones floating on the surface of our minds, in our conscious state.

In order to begin applying the Law of Attraction in a way that is fruitful, the first step is to understand what it is that we need, and what are the things that we desire that have the capacity to give us inner peace. You have to be able to filter out the deep-seated thoughts, beliefs, and desires that are hiding within the subconscious mind and bring them to the forefront of your thought process so that they become embedded in your mind as you go about your day.

IDENTIFY & PRESERVE POSITIVE COGNITION

It can get a bit confusing and can prove to be a little difficult to be confident in knowing what the 'right' thoughts to hold on to should be. You need to be able to identify a thought and work through it to really see whether it provokes positivity and strength in you, or whether it can take you to a darker place in your mind. Memories and flashbacks can be deceptive in that they can seem to be harmless enough but may hold negative implications for you. Some may remind you of insecurities or take you back to an unstable time in your life. If you come across a thought like this, it is important to know that this needs analysis and work but is not a thought that should be held for the use of the Law of Attraction just yet.

You want positive cognitive activity to be the priority, to begin with so that you are able to attract what you desire, believe, and need. Once you have established this, then you will be able to revisit the thoughts that you need to work through to turn a negative into a positive.

In order for this to be effective, you need to focus your positive energy on your subconscious to bring forward the good, humble, and encouraging thoughts that you are certain will support your beliefs. In turn, you'll be able to manifest energy that is simple and strong with positive vibrations.

THE POWER OF REPETITION, THE POWER OF SUGGESTION

We already understand how conditioning has worked throughout our upbringing. When you were an infant, your parents and caretakers knew that the best way to normalize an action or behavior was through repeating it countless times till it became a part of 'you' and your routines and habits. Later on in life, when you finally started having the capacity to think your own thoughts, the concept of suggestion began to take effect. Family, friends, and even influencers in your life, such as your teachers or coaches, all took to using the power of suggestion in order to sway you towards an idea or an action.

With the Law of Attraction, these two concepts can be used on a deeper level to help you manifest your desires in a smooth and effective way. After you have tapped into your subconscious and have identified the thoughts that you feel will help you move forward, the next step is to concentrate on repeating these thoughts as often as you can, until they become a natural part of your thought process. Implementing these desires and thoughts as suggestions, so that play into your actions is just as effective.

For example, let's say that one of your desires is to start writing. The first action is to repetitiously think, 'I love to write, I want to write, I need to write.' Then you can implement the desire in a suggestive way to link them to actions. You see a car you like, you observe a person doing something very mundane and normal, but you begin to suggest to yourself, 'If I love, want, I need to write, how about I write something about this car? Write about this person looking at an apple and imagine what kind of life they have?'

These actions are simple but are so incredibly effective, because they are easily brought into your routine train of thought and are the most natural way to manifest your desires and to keep the Law of Attraction as a way of life for you.

SELF-DISCIPLINE & AWARENESS

As we have mentioned earlier, the number of thoughts we have in all levels of consciousness are endless. In order to really be able to narrow down what kind of cognition is right for you, it is absolutely crucial that you apply focus on the filtration process.

Self-discipline and awareness go hand in hand. One complements the other in being able to apply the Law of Attraction to your thought process and subsequently, your overall energy output.

Self-Awareness: Being self-aware is being able to hone in on the ability to realize how your thoughts affect your feelings and actions. You are able to perceive your own emotions in a way that is observational and almost as if someone else were assessing them. Self-awareness comes with practice, and there is absolutely nothing wrong with seeking professional help from a life coach or therapist to help guide you on your quest to becoming more self-aware. To break it down even further, and to help you identify when you have truly become self-aware, you should be able to do these four things:

1. Identify the triggers and thoughts that cause negative feelings, such as stress and anxiety.

2. Identify the triggers, activities, and thoughts that give you positive energy.

3. Converse with and observe others without judgment.

4. Aim to resolve conflicts rather than escalate them.

Self-Discipline: Once you have mastered the art of being self-aware, you are now able to access your thoughts on both a conscious and subconscious level. The trick now is being able to master the art of self-discipline in order to know and understand how to filter and categorize the thoughts. By having the discipline to do this, you will be able to have a more organized thought process that will allow you to access thoughts at your beck and call.

Self-discipline does wonders for keeping the Law of Attraction working in a stable, strong, and consistent way as it teaches you how to deal with controlling your impulses, which play a huge role in the kind of energy and the level of vibrations you emit. It also teaches you about when the right time is to deal with negative or trying thoughts, and when to let go and bring forward your positive thoughts without having others conflict with it so that you are able to have a clear head at all times.

This is ideal of course, but it definitely takes practice, and you won't have it perfectly aligned all the time. But the more you focus on your self-awareness paired with your self-discipline and understand how the two work in cohesion, the more you will be able to emit the right kind of energy into the world. You will also become very competent in dealing with the thoughts that may be plaguing you, and learn how to turn them into positive energy instead of thoughts that bring you down and cloud your mind.

Understand the Purpose of your Desires

The point of the Law of Attraction is to attract and manifest our desire into our realities. So you now know how to align your thoughts in a way where you are capable of emitting the right kind of energy. But before you move forward with the process, you need to take a step back and think about what the actual *purpose* of your desire is.

Why do you have this urge or need- why do you desire its existence in your life? You need to jump a few steps forward and assume that you have achieved its presence in your life- what are the possible outcomes once it is prevalent in your life? How does it affect you as a person, your daily routine, the people around you, and your future?

There are many cases where you feel your desires but aren't entirely sure where the need comes from. The answer to this lies within you. This is why it is an ongoing process of growth to be able to access the material hidden deep within your subconscious. Look into your childhood and the stories behind your habits and lifestyle, and you'll be sure to find plenty of answers there. This way, you'll be able to find the substance that makes up the whole of why you have certain desires, and you'll have a better understanding of whether the outcome of achieving these desires will be positive or negative.

Looking at the big picture of who you are as a person makes you more aware of why you have certain desires, how they are connected, and what the ultimate goal should and will be. Understanding your desires makes it easier to apply the Law of Attraction because you understand what kinds of thoughts, energy, and vibrations will be thrown out into the universe, and more importantly, what you will receive in return.

The beauty of exploring your desires is that you may discover aspects of yourself that you never knew you had before. You may even run into a new way of achieving these things or discover even more enlightening factors along the way. Analyzing and assessing your desires is a journey in itself that helps to bring forth new perspectives.

You Attract What You Put Out

The core message of the Law of Attraction is that 'Like attracts like.' When you sum it up and simplify it, this is what it all comes down to. In many cases, this may seem easier said than done, but if you follow the processes that keep you aware that everything happens for a reason, then you will be able to overcome any trial and tribulation, and still come out on top because you managed to keep the positive outlook alive throughout your experiences.

It's as simple as this - a terrible event has occurred within the family, and everyone is upset and distressed. As a result, everyone is either in a foul mood or depressed. This, of course, is the natural reaction to something terrible happening. However, the effect of one person's smile and affection, their relentless positive outlook on life, can be contagious. This doesn't mean that this person does not feel the sorrow or the anger imposed by the event; it only means that they understand the purpose of their existence when such events take place. They understand by putting out positivity. They help others to move forward with a lighter feel and to accept what has occurred. They teach others around them that just as it is okay to feel bad about the event, it is imperative that they do not forget the importance of kindness, affection, and the strength that these characteristics give life to.

When you are able to harness the power of positivity and put it out into the world in a way that is non-imposing but rather, inviting and naturally flowing, you have reached the understanding of the true meaning of 'Like attracts Like.' All you need to do is put out your energy, and it's bound to attract that which is of similar or identical energy.

This applies to pretty much everything. Your thought process, when carried out correctly and has a purpose and goal in mind, is bound to attract anything you set your mind to.

Keep your Awareness Heightened

To utilize the power of the Law of Attraction completely, you need to keep your sense of awareness towards your thoughts, feelings, and emotions heightened. This means that your ability to send out the right kind of vibrations will be intact. But what does this really mean, and how can you do it?

Bob Proctor is someone who knows everything about vibrations and has spent many years teaching people how to activate their vibrations and keep them heightened. He goes in-depth about what the Law of Vibration really is, and why it's so important to the Law of Attraction.

The Law of Vibrations

Proctor brings to light that everything in this world, and the universe, exists and runs on energy. In everything you do, your brain cells activate and set up vibrations in your body that will dictate what you attract into your life. (Proctor, n.d.)

It's a given that there will be times where we will feel down, and as a result, our vibrations dive into their energy and strength. The best way to deal with this, in order to keep the level of the vibrations raised, is to confront the issues or triggers that are causing the drop or exposing yourself to things that help you relax or make you feel good. There are some universal options that are bound to work for everyone in the event that the vibrations need a little pick me up:

1. Listen to music: Music is the world's language for expression and altering the mood. By listening to your favorite music or soothing tracks, your vibrations will automatically be lifted.

2. <u>Remind yourself of what's important:</u> Think about all the wonderful things that you have in your life. Keeping a diary to note these things down so that you can go back to them with help raise your awareness and your vibrations.

3. <u>Get active:</u> When your vibrations are at an all-time low, get active, and do things that can raise your productivity. Being able to remain active with your mind and body, whether it be with a self-serving activity or one that serves the community, reminds you that you are worthy and this is all you need to keep your vibrations heightened. You will be able to have a sense of your purpose on this earth once again and realize the value of keeping your vibrations alive.

It's important that you keep your awareness of your thoughts and feelings in check at all times and as often as you can so that you are able to send out the right vibrations. The Law of Attraction relies on energy and vibrations, and once you have that down, you can't really go wrong.

Affirmation

Affirmation plays a significantly huge role when it comes to getting consistent results with the Law of Attraction. It may sound like a simple concept, but its effectiveness in affecting your energy and vibrations is proof enough of how important it is.

For someone that is new to the world of the Law of Attraction, sometimes finding the right positive affirmations that are actually convincing and effective is not always an easy feat. Self-affirmation is the act of repeating certain phrases to yourself in order to pick up your spirits and help you believe in yourself, your cause, purpose, and, of course, your desires. While this is the key to putting out the right vibrations to bringing your desires to life, it can be a struggle to believe the things you say to yourself if you have doubts in your mind. This is only natural, and all it takes is a bit of practice and perseverance in order to really get into the hang of it and have it become an effective tool for the Law of Attraction.

There are a couple of things that will make this process go down much more smoothly:

1. <u>Make a list:</u> Writing is the key to almost getting anything across your mental barriers. This is the

best way to experiment with different affirmative lines to see what hits the spot for you. It will also help clarify what it is that you would like to manifest. Make them short and simple so that they are easy to remember and clear in their intent.

2. Start & finish your day with an affirmation: While there is no set rule as to which time is best for applying self-affirmation, it makes sense to make it a rule for yourself that you wake up to positive affirmation, and that you put yourself to sleep repeating these mantras. Getting them in as many times as possible is always the best advice as it just reminds you of your self-worth and your goals.

3. Categorize your affirmations: It's a very good idea to have a different self-affirmation phrase for the different desires that you would like to manifest and do so by categorizing them so that the needs are clear and that you are also able to prioritize and see which desires need the most attention.

4. This is for what you want: It may feel a bit unnatural at first to supply your mind with messages that are not a part of your reality as yet.

But always remember that you need to repeat positive affirmations for the things that you want to come your way. You may not have them at present, but if you believe in it enough, send out the energy, vibrations and speak the affirmations, it will come to you.

Affirmation is a small daily act that will go a long way in keeping the wheels turning in your quest to manifest your desires, and plays a huge role in making the Law of Attraction a normal way of life for you.

As A Token
of My Gratitude...

Here is a **<u>FREE</u>** video training course on how to develop
Relentless Optimism

Positive thinking is a state of mind that naturally expects a positive outcome to events. Not all of us were born to be positive thinkers. The good news is that this mindset is a habit <u>that can be developed and enhanced</u>.

The benefits are greater happiness and the increased likelihood that you will be able to achieve whatever goals you create for yourself. Positive thinking knows no limits, while negative thoughts only create limitations.

Click the picture of the DVD box or navigate to the link below to claim your copy now!

https://tinyurl.com/RelentlessOptimism

CHAPTER 3

Key Steps to Manifesting your Dreams

Now that most of the theoretical material has been covered, and you have a solid understanding of what the Law of Attraction is and how it can work for you just as well as it has for many other people, the next step we need to cover is what it is you can do to begin the manifestation of your dreams and desires.

All of the steps that are needed to be taken are all connected and will flow together in order to help you realize your needs and dreams in a way that feels natural, and that will become second nature with the passage of time.

Clarify & Specify Your Desires

It's important that you open up to yourself and not hold back in finding within yourself what your hopes, dreams, desires, and needs may be. You'll never really know what it is you truly need to manifest in your life to make you a better person if you do not expose every detail to yourself first. You then need to filter your way through them all in order to find the desires that you *should and need* to manifest.

What Makes an Effective Desire?

Assess the life you are living now, and identify where you struggle the most.

- Are you financially unstable?

- Are you unhappy in your job/relationship?

- Are you lonely?

- Do you live an unhealthy life?

These are the kinds of questions that you need to be asking yourself to understand how to reach an effective desire. Once you have clarified what your life is lacking, look into the things that you *do* have. This way, you will be able to balance the good with the bad in your life and truly understand the missing link that you need.

An effective desire is one that is attainable with changes that you are capable of making. If you desire more money, are you willing to sit down and really think about what you are passionate about? You have to instill perseverance and discipline in order to take the risk of leaving your job and pursuing your dream. If you are passionate about what you do, it is bound to become a success.

Is your desire relevant to a more personal side of your life? Analyze the situation that you are currently in and try to look at it from the outside. You have to come to terms with the reality that any kind of unhappiness that is a result of personal relationships needs self-assessment. Is the person you are with toxic, or are you not putting in your best effort, if so, then why not? Once you come to terms with the facts of why you may be unhappy in a relationship, or if you are lonely and depressed, you will be able to assert the right kind of desire in order to move on and lead a healthier life. It is important to find inner peace and self-love before allowing people into your life.

Do you feel like you have no control over your vices? All of us have our guilty pleasures, but in many cases, these guilty pleasures become escape mechanisms and get out of hand. You need to understand what it is that you are escaping from, to begin with. Is it a negative childhood experience that has stuck with you throughout your life? Is it a trauma you have experienced that has caused deterioration? You have to first come to terms that the things you are running to as shelter from your thoughts are only plaguing them more and destroying you and your mind. Then the next step is going to be difficult- you will have to confront the core issue. It is advisable to seek guidance from a therapist or a life coach because, in most of these cases, it is a difficult process to go through. Once you are able to get through all of this, you will be able to identify the right desire to manifest. In this case, you will be able to formulate the right desire to invite the right kind of people and environment into your life.

Techniques & Exercises for Refining Desires

There are certain exercises and techniques that you can utilize to make the refining process go a lot smoother. In order to clarify the details of your desires, it's important for you to have a clear head. Focusing on the wrong desires is easy to do when you are stressed and feeling a collection of emotions. Following these steps will ensure that you make the right choice.

- **KEEP A DIARY**: Keep a diary only for recording your thoughts and feelings. This will help you narrow down what it is that you might need in your life. Being able to go back and read over what your thought process is over a period of time helps in pinpointing the true desires to focus on.

- **COUNT YOUR BLESSINGS:** If we are not aware of what we *do* have and only focus on what we *don't* have, applying desires incorrectly is bound to happen. Yes, of course, we have to be honest with ourselves and realize our needs unapologetically, but we need to do it wisely so that we do only good things for ourselves. Keep track of all of the wonderful things you have in your life, big and small. This way, you're bound to make a couple of revelations and even eliminate some desires because you will realize that you already have things available right in front of you- you just didn't acknowledge their existence. By doing this, you'll be able to reach your true desires.

- **BE HUMBLE, BE REAL:** It is very easy to get carried away in visualizing the things and the kind of life we desire. This is why it's important to constantly remind yourself of the importance of staying humble in order to stay true to yourself. Anything in excess is bound to bring in drama and complication, which only means unhappiness, and this is not something anyone desires to have in their lives. Understand the core principles of what it is you need to have inner peace and a comfortable life, and focus on those desires that will attain these things for you.

- **PHYSICAL EXERCISE:** Going for long walks or even going for a swim allows you to be alone with your thoughts and to be able to process them with a clear head. This is a great way to get your circulation pumping and the wheels in your mind turning in a way that will help you narrow down the right desires to focus on.

- **MANIFESTATION SCRIPTING:** Manifestation scripting is the process of writing out the script of your life the way you would ideally *want* it to be. This helps in clarifying your desires because it paints the full picture, with all the details. By doing this, you get to use your imagination, have fun, dream big, and most importantly, draw out a map of your life of how it may be. This way, you can pick out any impending issues or figure out things that you need to do.

- **MEDITATION**: Meditation is a great way to clear your mind of all the clutter that everyday stress builds upon it. If you make it a part of your daily routine to meditate once in the morning and right before going to bed, this will help in pinpointing the right desires. There are 2 kinds of meditation that you need to be aware of:

1. Mindfulness Meditation- The goal of this kind of meditation is to be able to observe your thoughts as they are fleeting. It's almost like you're watching from a window and seeing what these thoughts look like without getting involved in them.

2. Concentration Meditation- This kind of meditation works with the power of repetition. Once your head is clear, and you are focused, you repeat the affirmation like a mantra, and it enters a clear head in a much more effective way.

It is even sometimes advisable to practice both kinds of meditation together in order to really get the full effect of the concentration and the practice. Meditation is a wonderful way to discover thoughts and delve into the subconscious. It is also an effective tool in applying affirmation directly to the subconscious, which is much stronger than just using it consciously.

- **HYPNOSIS:** You will recall how an effective public figure in the world of Law of Attraction, Victoria Gallagher, specialized in Hypnotherapy long before she discovered the Law of Attraction. This is no coincidence, as the two go hand in hand extremely well.

Hypnosis is the act of being induced in a state of altered consciousness. It allows you to let your guard down and access your subconscious memories and thoughts with the help of a hypnotherapist. It is advisable that you consult a professional hypnotherapist that is familiar with the Law of Attraction so that they can help guide you through your subconscious. By doing so, you'll be able to access many hidden and buried images and thoughts that can really make a world of difference in your manifestation process. You will be able to have a better understanding of where the roots of your issues stem from and build upon why you may desire or need certain things. This way, it will make clarifying your desires and moving in the right direction much easier. Not only that but with guided hypnotherapy, you'll be able to work through traumas and any other negative feelings that have been harboring within your subconscious mind.

Once you have been able to get through this initial stage, your hypnotherapist will be able to help you use your scripting in order to reach you on a deeper level.

- **Self-Hypnosis:** This is the process of putting yourself into a hypnotic state so that you have access to your subconscious, or to simply put you in a more relaxed state of mind.

You can learn how to do this after you've been through guided hypnosis a couple of times so that you *know* what kind of state of mind you are trying to achieve, first and foremost. You also need to know that what is different about self-hypnosis is that there still needs to be a part of you that is conscious in order to do it, so you will not be able to experience as deeply as you would with guided hypnosis. There are actually a number of apps available that you can download on your phone or even videos that you can find online that can help you do this by yourself.

Self-hypnosis and meditation go hand in hand. As you meditate, you pretty much put yourself in a state of semi-hypnosis in order to access your subconscious. After attending a couple of guided hypnosis sessions, you will understand the way your mind is meant to feel when you have reached that state of mind where you are able to think clearly and access images and thoughts that have been hidden away for ages.

The reason why hypnosis is such a critical factor for the Law of Attraction is that through it, we are able to overcome the part of our mind and thoughts that are critical. This area of our consciousness plays on judgments and functions on the conditioning that we were exposed to as we grew up. Through hypnosis or self-hypnosis, we bypass that state and are able to access and eventually alter the thoughts in the subconscious mind, which will contribute greatly to the adjustment of your perception. Using repetitious affirmation whilst in this state is highly effective.

There is even scientific research that has been carried out to understand the effects of hypnosis better. One of the most interesting ones was conducted by Dr. Amir Raz in 2005, where he carried out a study to show how brain behavior changed when exposed to suggestion through hypnosis. He used the premise of the Stroop Effect. This is when the mind identifies takes longer to identify something because there is a mix up in stimuli. The famous example is writing the names of color, and having them written in a different color. For example, writing the word 'YELLOW' but it is written with red ink. As a result, our minds take longer to identify the correct answer because it is conditioned to have certain things set out in certain ways. (Raz, Kirsch, Pollard, & Nitkin-Kaner, 2005)

What Dr. Raz did was hypnotize his subjects and conducted the same test on them, informing them that there would be random words, sometimes ones that made no sense, and that they would have to identify the color. The results were very interesting as the subjects had no difficulty focusing on the request at hand. Their brain activity showed that they immediately focused on the instruction given to them under hypnosis and did not falter as they would in a conscious state, trying to figure out the words or their meanings, rather than what they were asked to do- which was to merely identify the color. Basically, the area in the brain that works to identify words was not even activated.

This proves that it is possible for the human mind to focus on what it *needs* using hypnosis rather than every single stimulus that is presented to us in any given situation. So you are very capable of training your mind to focus on what you need in order to reach your goals.

The practice of hypnosis has become so popular over time because many within the medical community have come to discover how effective it is in treating patients. This is particularly effective because they have realized that while in a hypnotic state, the mind is open to suggestion, and this makes it much easier to calm the mind and even infiltrate action to fight off pain. Some clinics use it for pain management, combatting depression, anxiety, and even addiction. This means that even you, within the comfort of your own home, are very capable of treating yourself of whatever may be plaguing your thoughts and stopping you from moving forward in your life.

Planning & Goal-Setting

The next step you need to take is to make sure that you map out a plan for the goals that you would like to reach. In order to be able to manifest with conviction, you need to know in detail what it is that you would like to achieve in your life, but before going into the details, list out the desires that stand out the most for you. There are bound to be needs and desires that stand out more than others.

It can be easy to become overwhelmed in this process, so it's important to stay organized. It's advisable that you separate and categorize these goals into short and long term goals, and consider using charts to make the visual more accessible for you. It's also important to assign yourself time frames to get these tasks done. Otherwise, the planning could get quite messy and confusing.

- <u>Short Term Goals:</u> Making plans for short term goals are the best to start with because it helps you to ease into the process and won't prove to be overwhelming. There are things that we need to do in our lives that are as simple as selling furniture and redoing a room, but once it's done, you'll be amazed at the sense of accomplishment that follows. Think about all of the little things that you have meant to do but have put off for some reason or the other, and add them to your schedule.

Start off with tasks that you are familiar and comfortable with, and then go a step further and begin assigning yourself short term goals that are out of your comfort zone. It may be a little scary at first, but once you do it, you won't look back. A good example is signing yourself up for a class that specializes in something that you've always dreamed of learning but never had the chance or courage to take up.

- <u>Long Term Goals:</u> Try to set up a realistic time frame when planning for long term goals as these fulfill the much more intricate desires of stability that you may need. Things such as having the security of owning your own home, leaving your job to start your own business, traveling to a country that you've never been to before for a certain amount of time, and so on.

Long term goals generally have details that need to be taken care of before you're able to reach that goal, so it's always a good idea to sit down and assess your long terms goals to see what needs to be done in order to attain them, and by doing this, you'll be able to have a vague idea of how long it should take.

- <u>Methods of organizing the goals:</u> There are a couple of ways in which you can display the planning of your goals so that you are constantly reminded of what they are and when you plan to have them manifested.

1. **Create a chart**- Have a huge chart made with your goals set on it. Split them into categories and try to have them within approximate time frames. Fill it up with pictures, ideas, any dreams, and desires. The idea of creating a vision or dream board has proven successful for many people. Its purpose is to create a source of inspiration and motivation to attain your goals.

2. **Goal Setting Apps** - Since we live in the age of technology, it would only make sense to have your goals put into a goal-setting app. This is extremely convenient because you have your smartphone with you at all times, and it's amazing that you are able to carry your goals with you wherever you go.

The Value of Affirmations

We can easily underestimate the value and effectiveness of self-affirmations. It is not merely the act of repeating phrases to oneself- there is much more going on when you make self-affirmation a part of your life.

After discovering what it is that you desire, and finding the goals that you want to reach, whether they be short or long term, the next step is to create self-affirming phrases that are personal to you, your journey, and your goal.

Using these phrases do wonders in all kinds of situations. For example, if you find yourself in a scenario where someone is verbally attacking you- even worse, in a way that is indirect- this is bound to do serious damage to your self-esteem, and you cannot help but question your self-worth. You know that the long term solution is to cut this toxic person out of your life, but what is the solution in that very moment?

At the back of your head, you need to have the affirmation that this person does not define you, does not know you, and cannot hurt you with their words, because they are not true- even if they believe it to be so. Knowing that you will undoubtedly be faced with aggressive confrontations in your life helps you to prepare beforehand. Having the self-affirming phrases at the ready, for any kind of situation, protects your self-esteem and your self-worth. Take the time to imagine any kind of scenario under the sun, and create a couple of phrases that you can either have written in a trusty notebook or your phone in your bag, or have a huge board at home where you can keep pinning up any affirmation you think of so that it's right in front of you whenever you're in the kitchen or the bedroom, for instance.

How to Utilize These Steps

It may seem like a lot to do initially, but if you take each step at a time, and take your time with it, you'll find that it will flow very naturally within your daily routine. There's really no die-hard rules as such because we cannot forget that this is the process of implementing change within you or your thought process, and essentially, your life and lifestyle. If it is applied in a boot camp kind of way, then it is bound to fall apart at some point.

With the Law of Attraction, the journey is about self-discovery more than anything else. These are simply steps to *guide* you. You need to explore all the different methods that allow you to tap into your subconscious thoughts, treat your ailments, and discover your true desire. Try everything until you find the way that works best for you, although you'll be sure to find that each step serves a separate purpose that will be beneficial to you.

Never stop with the affirmation- these can change as you grow, and will never cease to be helpful in fulfilling your desires and protecting your moral ground and your self-worth.

We all have to learn that there is no shame in asking for help. That, in fact, it is admirable that you are brave enough to show your vulnerability and that you are willing to humble yourself. It's important to do so if you are to ever move forward in realizing your desires and start to apply the Law of Attraction in a way that is everlasting. Seek out professional help- whether it be a therapist, a hypnotherapist, or even a life coach. Research and read about different people's experiences with the Law of Attraction, as this will only encourage you to stay strong on your path of transformation.

Learn how to access your subconscious so that you are able to get to know yourself on a different level. Many times, you will find it difficult to confront certain memories or revelations about your past or your current situations, and that's okay. Never forget that this is how we begin the healing process, and the healing only leads to growth. Meditation is a wonderful way to detach from the world and delve deep inside your mind. Discovering new triggers, new thoughts, and memories will allow you to understand your path and your ultimate goal even better. Read more! Read more on different forms of meditation, the Law of Attraction, the history of the world, and the different religions of the world. The list is endless, and knowledge is power. The more you read, the more you discover about how people think and how they work, and how this may affect you ultimately.

In order to turn your life around, sometimes, you may have to make difficult choices. You need to take a good long hard look at your environment and the people that surround you. You need to be honest with yourself in terms of identifying where you need to work on yourself, but also what you need to eliminate from your life. Toxic people are the most poisonous thing for your soul, and in order to be whole again, you must wish them well, and let them go. If you live in a setting that makes it difficult for you to break out from a negative cycle, then it's time to seriously consider moving. You will only be able to break free of the shackles that bind your mind if you break free from the surrounding environments that create and control your negative lifestyle and thoughts.

It's going to be an exciting journey, and it may be a bit trying at times, but it will always be fulfilling. Knowing that you took control of your destiny is something that you will never regret. Having guidance and a support network is crucial when you begin this new journey through the Law of Attraction, and you're never alone because there's a world out there waiting for you to reach out and grab it, make it your own. Following these steps will help you get started on a journey that you have been waiting to take all your life. These steps will also help you stay on track as they are easy to integrate into your daily life naturally. The Law of Attraction is a way of life, a lifestyle, and a mode of thought that will bring you to your best self yet.

SECTION 2

WRITING THAT IMPACTS THE SUBCONSCIOUS & MANIFESTS

CHAPTER 4

Writing Formats for Manifesting

We have gone through the processes necessary to *think* and *feel;* but now comes the process of manifestation and action. You may be wondering why writing, in particular, is the medium of expression chosen for manifestation. From the beginning of time, we, as humans, have sought to express our feelings and tell our stories through writing, in order to etch them into our minds and to leave behind a record of our history.

When it comes to the Law of Attraction, nothing influences your energy and vibrations more than actually visualizing your hopes, dreams, and aspirations. And the best way to do that in a way that you can go back and alter or even just remind yourself of it is to write. Writing is a personal and expressive exercise that unfortunately, many of us in this generation have underplayed. It is truly a lost art that needs to be revived. Putting pen to paper is almost like holding a magic wand to bring your thoughts to life, or a secret weapon to destroy all your fears and insecurities.

There are a couple of writing formats available that you should try out to apply the Law of Attraction, in order to practice processing your desires and manifesting them the best and the most organized way possible. It is advisable to also do it in the order mentioned below because this will help you to attain maximum benefits from the order of the process in applying the Law of Attraction to your life.

Journaling

There are very few that haven't had the experience of keeping a journal as a kid. Getting your first diary was a cause for celebration. Whether it was a normal notebook or one of those with a lock on it, it made you feel like you had a forbidden treasure in your possession. That you could finally share your deepest darkest secrets without having to worry about whether they would be shared or not because your diary was the safest place to go.

In terms of how this helps in having the Law of Attraction become a part of your life, journaling is extremely effective. There are a couple of ways for you to journal, and it's never a bad idea to give each kind a shot to see which one you are comfortable with and which works out for you best in the manifestation process.

• **The Daily Journal**

Having a notebook that is exclusively assigned to recording the daily occurrences that take place is important for a number of reasons.

-You become aware of your demeanor. Do you have a positive or negative outlook on how the events in your life unfold? This is a wonderful way to make realizations and assessments in order to work towards a better life.

-You start to notice that many things that bother you are not worth the attention you give them. We tend to get sucked into daily events and gossip that clouds our judgment and takes our attention away from our true purpose. The Law of Attraction comes into play when you begin to realize what it is you need to let go.

-Patterns in your behavior are easier to recognize. You will also be able to identify the people in your life that bring positivity and those who prove to be toxic once you re-read your entries and discover who contributes to which emotions that you experience throughout your day.

- **The Journal of Gratitude**

You need to have a separate notebook for this so that it is easy for you to differentiate between the stream of events occurring throughout your day from your normal journal, and how to identify the things that you are actually grateful for through the gratitude journal.

When you start the journal of gratitude, it might prove to be a little difficult at first, especially if you're having a particularly difficult day. And this is why it is something that you have to commit to daily so that you can get the hang of it and have it become a natural off-loading process.

No matter how hard or stressful your day has been, you must find the good in it. And the reality is, there is always good, even in the worst of situations. So after you are done with you normal daily journal, where you let all lose, be sure to turn to your gratitude journal and find and express the things that you were grateful for that happened on this very day. You'll be surprised to find that there are plenty of lessons in every incident that occurs in your life, and every lesson has the power of good; it is just a matter of perspective. The Law of Attraction begins to take effect once you are able to train your mind to naturally seek the good in every kind of situation. Not only will you find strength in your ability to perceive positively, but you will also end up giving off positive vibrations as a result.

5 Minute Journaling for Effective Gratitude

Although many people create a bullet-point journal for listing what they're grateful for the most, there are other templates that you can follow to help jumpstart your writing habits. Try these daily journaling templates:

5 Minute Day Journal:

- I'm grateful for:

1. _____

2. _____

3. _____

- What would make this day truly great?

1. _____

2. _____

3. _____

5 Minute Night Journal:

- What 3 wonderful things happened today:

1. _____

2._____

3._____

- How could I have worked towards making today better?

1. _____

2._____

3._____

Affirmation

We have mentioned and explained what affirmation is in previous chapters. Now it's important for you to know *how* you can discover the right self-affirmation within yourself. You can do this by using writing as an effective and consistent tool, that grows with you as you proceed through the stages of self-discovery through the Law of Attraction.

After you are done with your daily entries in both your normal and gratitude journals, read over what you have written. What would you like to change in your circumstances? Would you like to leave your job because you're unhappy with the environment? Then the affirmation statement for you is "I will work hard to find new avenues," "I will not allow negative energy to bring me down," "I am in control of my mental well-being," and so on. Keep a notebook that you can carry around in your bag, as well as a whiteboard or just a board where you can post notes on that have these statements written on them so that they are in your face and in your mind as often as possible.

Just to give you a head start, we're going to provide some examples of self-affirmative quotes that you can use for different situations:

- I am strong enough to get through the day.

- Today will be a good day because I will make it good.

- If I work hard, I will win big.

- I won't let anyone's negativity affect me today.

- Something amazing will happen to me.

- Treat others the way I'd like them to treat me.

- Everything happens for a good reason.

- I am worthy, no matter how anyone makes me feel otherwise.

- The Law of Attraction is within me, and I will succeed.

- There is knowledge in every challenge I face.

- The energy I put out is what I will receive.

- I will learn something new today. I will do something memorable.

- Every problem is an opportunity to learn something new and grow stronger.

The key to really having the affirmation take effect is, as mentioned earlier, the power of repetition and suggestion. Repetition allows us to overcome any doubts we may have about the given statement, and actually helps you to believe in yourself and your ability to achieve your desires. Suggestion is the best way to introduce ideas and actions that you need to take on in order to make new steps and introduce new perceptions that will ultimately lead you to your goal and help you play the Law of Attraction to its best powers.

The key to really having affirmations delve deep into your soul and really have an influence on you in a way that helps you change and apply the Law of Attraction is to discover and create statements that relate to you on a personal level. If they are merely words that you copied from somewhere, chances are, you may find you relate somewhat, but it may be too vague. If this is the case, its effectiveness may not be as powerful as the Law of Attraction requires. This is why it's so important that you get through your journaling and really assess it to find what it is that's missing, what you desire, what you need, and what words really move you the most.

This is why writing is so important. Through writing, we are able to discover words and expressions that touch something in our souls and help us reach new heights with the Law of Attraction through new perspectives.

Writing Affirmations

Now that we've given you an idea of what kind of affirmations to say and how to say it, it's time for you to start writing your own. Start off by writing a description of yourself and the way you want to be. Take some time to think it through and ask yourself if you want to be more courageous, more intellectual, or more outgoing. Start with your qualities first, and then move onto your habits.

<u>Qualities</u>

List five to ten qualities about yourself that would contribute to your success and that you would like to be part of the ideal you. Start with "I am," state the quality or attitude you desire, then use statements that expand or exemplifies your new quality. Be specific!

For example: "I am creative. I have great ideas and pursue them confidently and vigorously."

1. _____

2. _____

3. _____

4. _____

5. _____

6. _____

7. _____

8. _____

9. _____

10. _____

<u>Habits</u>

List five to ten daily habits that you would like to be part of the ideal you, and this can only happen when you know who you want to be. Each affirmation should start with "I am." It should also include an adverb and a strong verb. Be specific!

For example: "I am joyously playing with my children for an hour at least three times a week."

1. _____

2. _____

3. _____

4. _____

5. _____

6. _____

7. _____

8. _____

9. _____

10. _____

Manifesting Script

Writing out a manifesting script is pretty much you writing out a script of the life you long to have. It's like writing out the plan of your future just the way you foresee it to be, assuming that everything goes the way you plan it. It may seem a little odd at first. But think of it this way- you're writing the story of your life, or you're entering a make-believe world that has the prospect of being reality. The point is, you're writing it as if this is something that has already occurred - you're writing the story of your life as if you are watching it unfold. If this process feels weird or you have no idea where to start, don't worry. There are ways in which this process will actually come to you very naturally, and you'll end up having a lot of fun with it.

All you need are a couple of blank pieces of paper, a pen, your good vibes, and your imagination. The most important thing to remember is that this is supposed to be an enlightening and exciting exercise - not one that makes you dwell over every single image and scene and detail to the point where you are stressed.

If you would like to have some structure to the process- and you should- then try to take these factors into consideration as you write:

1. <u>Clarify what you desire</u>- By doing this, it becomes easier to plan out the script into sections or 'scenes' where you address the event and create it to get that specific desire.

2. <u>Understand the desire's purpose</u>- By understanding *why* you desire this particular thing or event to be a part of your life, it becomes easier to place it in a certain time frame and in which setting that it would be ideal to pursue and have.

3. <u>Live the experience through your words</u> - By writing out your life's script, you will be able actually to experience what your life will be like. How it will be different and how *you* will be different once that desire is fulfilled.

4. <u>Make it realistic </u>- It's wonderful to dream, and to dream big too! And although you should be having fun as you write your manifestation script, you also want it to be a script of your life as it unfolds. That is, you want to make it achievable. You can dream big, but be sure that when you do, you have enough to support achieving this dream in a way that puts the Law of Attraction to work in a more plausible way.

5. <u>Have a timeline </u>- As you proceed to implement the Law of Attraction into the story of your life, with all the things you want, need and desire, it only makes sense that you space out these milestones at specific times in your life. It doesn't have to be a set date as such, but it should have a vague window. For example, you can set deadlines for certain desires, such as buying your first car or your first home. If you want to leave your 9 to 5 desk job and start your own business, you need to have a plan for that and definitely work it out in a way where when you do start, you're still relatively young so that you have time to hustle and be active in getting this business off the ground.

6. <u>Keep a general and daily script</u> - There are no rules to say what you can and can't do with scripting. But to allow you to have a little bit more detail and organization, you should consider having two kinds of scripts.

    • GENERAL SCRIPT: A general script is one that you write to go over the length of your life. Either from beginning to end, or you can start from the present time, and move forward, or you can start a little ahead in the future to give yourself time to get prepared.

- DAILY SCRIPT: We've already talked about journaling and how it's important in the process of manifestation for the Law of Attraction to work. Applying the concept of scripting to a journal is also a brilliant idea. You should keep a separate diary for daily script keeping, and it's actually going to do wonders when you compare notes with your scripting diary and your day to day events. This is a great way to see the progress of how you are applying the Law of Attraction and how well it is working. Soon, you may find that there is not much difference between your normal journaling and your daily script!

Manifestation Journal/Outline

Manifestation Goal

●

How Does it Feel?

Milestones

●

●

●

●

●

What do I need?

Gratitude

-
-
-
-
-

Scripting Your Future

What's sacred to you?

(Use this space to describe what a sacred moment looks like for you. How would you like future moments to be? What missing elements would you incorporate?)

Brainstorm/Draft a Script

(Use this space to brainstorm how you envision the coming year would be like. What would you like to achieve? How would your financial situation be like? Love life? Career? Health? Write down as many categories as you can)

Visualization Exercise

This step is absolutely crucial to bringing together all the work you have done and collected in writing. Visualization exercises help you to apply images to your thoughts, desires, and affirmations. This is an important step in applying the Law of Attraction because, as humans, visual stimulation adds an extra dimension to any aspect. In terms of manifesting your desires, visual aid seals the deal in the sense that you can actually *see* your desires before your mind's eye, and it is that much closer to becoming a reality.

The term itself may seem intimidating and foreign. But if you really think about it, we've been visualizing since we were little children. When you used to daydream and use your imagination to think of imaginary people, animals, and situations, you were using the power of visualization. We take the inner creativity that we have lost as a child and bring it back to life through visualization, and take it up a notch with the application of the Law of Attraction.

Productive Visualization

Productive visualization is the adult version of daydreaming that has been upgraded and modified to help you manifest your desires. When we spoke about the power of suggestion earlier, this is a concept that helps to kick start the process of productive visualization.

What you have learned about accessing your subconscious all the way through to putting pen to paper to record your daily events, feelings of gratitude, as well as the affirmative quotes that you have collected- all of these things put together will allow your mind to finally see a visual rendition of what it is you want and need in order to move forward in a positive and effective way.

- Create a Space

It's important that right from the very first time, you set certain ground rules for yourself in order to be able to visualize productively and effectively. This is more defining than you think because your mind works off of triggers and habit. So if you train your mind to do a certain action or activity in a specific setting, soon enough, this will come without you even having to think about it actively; your subconscious takes the trigger and goes full speed ahead. This is why it is very important to implement a positive trigger to overcome the negative ones.

Start off by creating a physical space in your home that you can assign exclusively for everything related to your

Law of Attraction exercises. This will help you to focus better and collect your thoughts. As for how it specifically applies to the exercise of visualization, find a spot that is immersed in natural sunlight, and have a couple of plants placed in that spot that you feel give you serenity. Be sure to have as little as possible in that space - by having an actual visual of less clutter, your mind is encouraged to find less clutter and more clarity as well. You will realize the importance of sensory triggers in your space of focus and meditation once you become more seasoned in it. Smells, special values, inanimate objects - all of these contribute to how well you begin your visualization process.

- Meditation & Visualization

Through meditation, we have learned that we have better focus and ability to access the thoughts of our subconscious. What meditation can also help us do is conjure up images of these thoughts that are stored in the subconscious, as well as controlling these thoughts and images by integrating your self-affirming statements as you meditate.

Keeping your gratitude journal as well as your self-affirmation quotes by you as you go into a meditative state so that you have them as a reference and reminder of what it is you need to apply to your thoughts, and what images you need to manifest. By seeing the future of your desires coming alive as you meditate, you embed these images into both your conscious and subconscious state of mind. By doing so on a daily basis, it becomes easier for these images to become one with your thought process as you go about your day. This way, you are reminded of the goal on a subconscious and visual level. Your energy becomes vamped up, confident and positive, and before you know it, you are focused on retaining the Law of Attraction by having these vibrations going out into the world.

- Productive Visualization on the go

Getting the hang of visualization through meditation is the best way to start if you are new to this, as it teaches you how to really get into your own head. Once you understand how to visualize within the confines of your private space, you will be able to slowly integrate the ability to visualize productively anywhere you go.

When you find yourself faced with a stressful situation, for example, you can train your mind to access that peaceful place that you go to when you are meditating at home and visualizing. This can be done if you step away from the situation and find a moment to close your eyes and regulate your breathing so that you can balance your focus. Another way to cope with stressful situations is by conjuring up the images that you have practiced visualizing at home that remind you of the affirmative quotes and what you remember from your Gratitude Journal.

Besides applying productive visualization in times of stress, it's important that you do so as often as you can. You don't only want to control the stress entering your life, but ultimately, you want to use the Law of Attraction to bring your desires to life. And you can do that by consistently visualizing what you have worked on in your Manifestation Script.

CHAPTER 5

Transforming Others Through Powerful Writing

At this stage in the book, you should have grasped the main principles of the Law of Attraction. Thoughts are believed to evoke emotion, positivity, and clarity. When your thoughts have reached the highest levels of positive energy, you can become skilled enough in utilizing them in the power of transformation. Only when you have truly transformed yourself, can you transform others.

Becoming an author and penning your own transformational book requires authenticity and believability. You don't want to appear a fraud, after all. Not to mention the fact that if you don't believe yourself in what you're convincing others with, then it will never take the form of a believable reality or authentic thoughts on paper. And this is when you need to take advantage of your expertise.

Your life experience can make you an expert; what you learned, what you faced, and what you have accomplished can help others going through the same things. We're not all that different if you think about it; anyone has the power to affect at least one person. But first, you have to understand yourself and what you want to write about.

No matter what style you adopt, be it a journal, an essay, a blog post, a memoir, or a transformational story, it's a great way to digest your own feelings and understand them from a different and much broader perspective. There are many teachings that authors relay onto those who wish to become future writers themselves. The first one is to *show, don't tell.* And we will discuss this further on in the chapter and how you can create imagery for believability.

The second teaching is to *write what you know*. Writing can be a very personal and intimate activity; when you write, you reach deep inside your thoughts, your experiences, your beliefs, and you find the right words to draw them onto paper. "Writing one's story is a way to reclaim your voice… and gain a deeper understanding of one's place in the world." (Raab, 2017) When you reclaim your voice, you can use it in the transformational power of language and storytelling to make your voice heard and your message loud and clear.

Defining Transformational Writing

Transformational writing exists by using one's own experience to inspire change, whether personal or societal. It's designed to heal, to transform, and to allow one to go through a path of self-discovery. Anthropology sees transformational storytelling as a writing technique that aims to offer alternatives to the status quo. Artistically, writing is a craft, and the difference between writers is their power of storytelling.

Anyone can write an essay with the aim of inspiring only to fall flat because they weren't believable enough. But true, compelling narratives, brought from the depth of the writer's thoughts and experiences, are the ones that have the power to bring on change and inspire one to become the best versions of themselves. Compelling storytelling can educate the reader, open their eyes onto aspects of their life they couldn't see, adjust their perspective, and finally, inspire change.

Reframing Intentions for Believability

As mentioned before in this book, our brains are programmed to think of the negative before the positive. When you face an unpleasant experience, part of this unpleasant feeling might actually be internal and has nothing to do with any external factor. It's how you view this experience that counts. However, when you reframe your intentions and thoughts, you're changing the meaning of this experience in a way that allows you to adjust and rethink your initial response to it.

To reframe your thoughts, it means that you're seeing it in a different light and viewing it from another angle. You're placing it in a different context, setting, or frame. Changing your initial response to any experience will effectively reframe the experience itself. This, of course, correlates with your energy and vibrations. When you focus on your energy, you will alter your reality by just focusing on manifesting what you really want or feel.

Your words and thoughts can either elevate you or weaken you. At any given situation, your words, and the energy that is fueled through them, drastically affect how you feel. This is why it's highly necessary to become mindful of what we think and what we say to reframe our thoughts successfully. Which will then eventually be passed onto your writing.

The first thing you need to do is to take a step back and examine your thoughts. Have an internal monologue with yourself daily. You can even use a journal to write down some of these thoughts; when they're on paper, it will allow you to inspect which words or situations that are creating negative vibes in your life. Become fearlessly honest with yourself to find out what's truly blocking you from reaching positivity and joy. Ask yourself the following:

- What stories or experiences weaken your energy?

- What intentions lower your physical, spiritual, and emotional experiences?

- How are your words or thoughts affecting you and the people around you?

- Are your words and thoughts holding you back from being confident and inspired?

Answer these questions honestly, and you can empower your intentions by using these thoughts, words, and energy through proper inspection and reflection. You do not want to just change the words, but how you *feel* when they are spoken, as well as how they affect you. You have to believe in the energy created by your words because once you being reframing your thoughts and intentions, you'll notice that there is a significant shift in energy and a sudden lift in your vibrations.

Consider this hypothetical situation to make the idea of reframing your thoughts more clear. Let's say you work in a field where you have to meet a lot of potential clients over dinner or drinks to make a sale, for example. However, you're a person who doesn't like to drink too much. During the evening meeting, it runs long because you're chatting away with your clients and answering every possible question or concern they have. They order drinks and so do you, more than you would have liked. Naturally, you end the night regretting how you couldn't control your drink intake and believe that you've "wasted" your time. However, when you start examining the night and what really happened, you should be able to notice that "chatting" with said clients is an attempt to build a bond and a relationship of trust with them. This in itself improves your chances of making your sale or whatever business task required. The night wasn't a waste after all. Examining your thoughts and your intentions will make you understand more the positive intent of drinking, and you'll be more open to seeing this experience in a different and positive perspective.

Reframing Techniques

- **Moment-to-Moment Practice:**

Reframing your thoughts might sound easier said than done. But as they say, practice makes perfect. In her book, *Mirrors Now,* author Gabrielle Bernstein believes that when you choose to practice daily or a moment-based practice of reframing your thoughts and intentions, it will eventually come as second nature to you. All you have to do is to develop this habit for it to succeed. Start paying attention to your worst thoughts that create negative energy, and consciously make an attempt to change them. (Bernstein, 2014)

You might occasionally fall back into your old habits when faced with an unpleasant situation, and that's okay. Be kind and compassionate to yourself; it's a process that needs time and patience. Make sure you celebrate each change you achieve because you're one step closer in elevating your vibrations. Fear is one way that will block out and prevent this change. Don't let your fear take charge, but take charge of your fear instead. We've been programmed to lean toward fear, so naturally, we do. But when you're more determined and proactive to lean toward positivity, joy, acceptance, and love, you'll begin to attract what you truly want and what you believe in.

This daily practice will drastically help you, even in dire situations. You might be struggling with your job, facing financial woes, maybe your marriage is ending, or you're battling a ruthless disease. Whatever keeps you up at night can be transformed when you organize your thoughts and intentions. In your darkest of moments, there's always a chance of spiritual surrender.

- **The W.A.I.T. Method**

We go through thousands of thoughts each day, and we tend to think that they are out of our control. However, we have the ability to take a step back, interrupt this stream of thought, and examine them. Ask yourself why you're having these thoughts and understand how they make you feel. One of the methods you can use is the W.A.I.T. method, which allows you to consciously steer what you're thinking in a different direction.

Basically, it stands for "Why am I talking?" You can use this method during the times you talk or think mindlessly, and most often than not, these are the moments that tend to bring you down. Once you notice words with negative connotations or words that bring you down whether in a conversation or in your head, ask yourself W.A.I.T. Then, take a breath and reframe your own thoughts and words into positive ones. Even if you stop mid-sentence, just recognize the fact that these words are bringing your energy down. (Bernstein, 2014)

The Six-Step Frame

Practitioners in Neuro-Linguistic Programming (NLP) have developed this method to help anyone reframe their own thoughts and intentions. Follow this strategy below for a much more effective reframing technique.

1.   Identify the problem in your behavior.

_____

_____

_____

_____

2.   Identify the positive intention behind the behavior

_____

_____

_____

_____

3.   Ask yourself if there are other ways of accomplishing positive intention and if you're interested in discovering them.

_____

_____

_____

_____

4.   Brainstorm other ways that you can handle a situation without letting your behavioral problem interfering.   Will   your   ideas   allow   for   better implementation of positive intention?

_____

_____

_____

_____

5.   Identify at least three new choices from your list that you prefer.

_____

_____

_____

_____

6.   Finally, examine any objections you have or assess your commitment level to the aforementioned plan.

_____

_____

_____

_____

Creating Imagery and Sensory Details

Any writer has heard the phrase *Show, don't tell* on so many occasions. And as much as it may feel redundant, it's actually a very important skill to master to make your book appealing to any reader. Using imagery or sensory details has always been a hallmark for any kind of writer, and it's what sets their book apart from a publisher's "slush pile." Consider these statements below as examples:

"The park was filled with people. Children called out to their parents, and the barking of a dog could be heard over the sounds of a ball game in the distance. The smell of freshly-cut grass was a nostalgic aroma as she flipped through the pages of her book, and the warmth of the sun on her hand made her smile."

As you were reading this sentence, did you picture it? Did you smell the grass or feel the warmth of the sun? Did you hear the children calling each other? If this sentence spoke to any of your senses, then that's because it's a descriptive one using sensory details to make you, as a reader, feel something in particular.

"The sound of birds singing fills the air. A soft breeze ruffles your hair. You watch the sun fall in rays between the gently dancing leaves."

In this sentence, the author uses strong imagery to paint a picture in the reader's mind. It's another technique to draw in the readers and give your words weight and meaning.

Imagery has been used for decades by many poets; Romantic ones like Wordsworth, Keats, and Shelley were considered masters of imagery. When using imagery, think of yourself as a photographer or a painter. Instead of showing the reader the image you have in mind, you tell it to them by creatively using your words. Paint them a word picture, as one would say. Imagery is a literary device that houses many writing techniques such as metaphors, similes, hyperbole, and personification, as to many others. Vivid imagery and figurative language will help make your words come alive on the page and will tickle your reader's imagination.

Sensory details speak to the five senses, consider them your best friend when writing figurative language. These details include words that appeal to the sense of sight, sound, smell, taste, and touch. They're descriptive to allow the reader to experience the world you've created on paper; you're allowing them to hear, to see, to smell, to touch, and to taste with your words.

At this point, you might wonder what sensory details or imagery have to do with writing a transformational book. You might even think that only novelists and poets use figurative language. On the contrary, any type of writer can use this writing technique to give meaning and power to their words. Writing by using sensory language can help you captivate any kind of audience because it allows the reader to experience the world you've created as if they're right in the middle of it. Sensory language also has the power to make any dull or mundane content much more interesting; it gives it a personality and flavor, helping you stand out in a sea of writers. This technique is ideal in writing transformational content because, in order to convince a reader with the power of change, you need strong words at your side.

The Science behind Sensory Language

Sensory words are more powerful than ordinary words and are processed differently by your brain. Research conducted by neuroscientists and psychologists has proven that the brain responds differently when a person is reading basic text as opposed to text that is filled with sensory language. Certain areas in the brain light up when reading metaphors because it speaks to our sensory-motor experience; therefore, we might get activity in the sensory parts of our brains. (Lacey, Stilla, & Sathian, 2012) Another study has claimed that the brain has the ability to understand and comprehend tangible or sensory words faster than other words, which also means that words have the power to evoke sensory and perceptual experiences in our brains. (Juhasz, Yap, Dicke, Taylor, & Gullick, 2011) For decades, writers have been taking advantage of that, possibly unknowingly, for its effect on the reader.

Figurative Language Tips

When using figurative language in your writing, the goal here is to allow your reader to clearly envision what's going on by subtly appealing to their senses without overwhelming them. These tips can help make your writing even more powerful.

Choose the right words: Choosing words without appearing corny or predictable will help make your message come across better. It's not just about choosing adjectives or vividly describing a situation; it has to also mean something great and complement the mood of your story.

Avoid clichés: There is a number of cliché imagery that has been used so many times by so many authors. Be different and stand out. When using the word white, you don't need to say it was as white as snow. The night doesn't need to be as dark as coal. And depression doesn't need to be dark, either. Have you thought of giving it an ironic twist? Or exaggerate what it can signify? Your goal here is to bring a new perspective to the mundane.

Don't stop: When writing, don't stop mid-description. Keep going. Expand your story to include your surroundings to bring a more holistic idea to the reader of what's going on. Incorporate your narrative within your description; don't just stop what you mean to say to describe. Include whatever dialogue or action you're using within the imagery.

Go beyond adjectives: To be effective with using sensory language, you can also use the right verb or noun to describe; don't restrict yourself to adjectives only. Use action-bearing cushioned verbs like absorbed or grasped.

Know when to use it: It's important that you don't overwhelm the reader, but you pique their interest as well. Use sensory language when it fits the situation you're writing about or when you're trying to get a message across. You may conjure all the senses, or you may only want to use one.

Sensory Language Exercises

- *Writing prompt 1*

Choose an object and make an attempt to describe it. First, describe how it looks like from all angles after carefully examining it. Then, close your eyes, feel it, and smell it. Write everything that you *feel* using sensory language. Keep your words flowing and write the first few things that come to your mind.

- *Writing prompt 2*

This prompt will allow you to attempt to describe an experience to someone who hasn't experienced it before. For example, try to describe the sunset to a visually-impaired person. Or describe how chocolate cake tastes to someone who hasn't tried it before. This will allow you to use descriptive words and imagery to make your audience understand the experience without actually going through it.

Considerations for plot, action, and characters

When you feel that you have transformed from one life situation to another or you feel you have overcome something powerful, more often than not, you would like to share this with others. Transformational writing, no matter what type of writing format you choose, requires you to do some soul-searching and find a need for why you're writing this. Is it to share how you overcame what you did and you're looking to inspire others to do? Is it to talk about a specific topic close to your heart with the need to help bring awareness to this topic? Are you planning to write about societal change? Whatever it is you wish to write about, make sure you're targeting the write audience, make sure it has an interesting plot and action, as well as a character that goes through the necessary transformation. You need to be able to address your topic in a different way; it needs to stand out among other books, not blend in with what's out there. Angle your book in a way that offers a solution to the problem you're writing about.

Your writing needs to be a wake-up call. It needs to be able to transform others in a way by sharing the light as well as how you got there out of the dark. It's a journey of healing, of improving, and of becoming the better version of yourself. You're passing on your knowledge of this topic and sharing your experience for others to learn from. This 'book in you' needs to show the grief, the shame, the tragedy, the tears, but it should also show the epiphanies, the strength, the will-power, the energy, and the determination. Your story can be the light at the end of the tunnel, waiting to benefit someone going through the same thing you have.

Developing a Character

Some of the best fiction or nonfiction out there is when the character changes in a significant and dramatic way. The best characters on television or in movies are the ones who have drastically developed and grown. In his book, *Plot Versus Character*, author Jeff Gerke believes that it speaks more to the audience when someone goes through a transformation, and they love and resonate with these characters. It's mainly because they're more human this way and it shows us that when they transform, *we* transform as well. (Gerke, 2010) We know how difficult it can be to transform, to give up our old ways, and to turn anew. And it's always uplifting to witness the journey the character makes, especially if success is waiting for them on the other side. And this is why character transformations or transformational writing matters.

In her book, *The Power of the Transformational Arc*, author Dara Marks believes that if any character or living being isn't evolving, then they're only moving towards death. It's cowardice not to face conflict and come out the other end a changed person. Any stories that don't reflect a real inner struggle can fall flat. (Marks, 2006) There needs to be a connection between the external factors as well as the inner struggle to make your story compelling. Internal struggles are what drives a person to take action. In order for stories to be compelling, it wouldn't work if one wrote about how a character approaches obstacles or takes on the heroic path just because he was born a hero. Where is the development in that? It's only when one faces challenges and is forced to on the path of self-discovery and personal growth would true transformation happen. This is how you can get your audience to engage, to learn what the character in your book is learning, and to feel transformed themselves.

Develop your character by keeping in mind these steps below:

1. Introduce your character early on: what's their name, what do they look like, any significant physical features, and so on.

2. Make the character memorable. Often at the beginning of a story, characters can be confusing. Avoid that by making your protagonist distinctive.

3. Give your character a backstory. It's always interesting to know what shaped this character to who they are today. What are their goals? Their dreams? Their world views?

4. Make sure that your protagonist is human, vulnerable, and flawed. It's impossible to identify with a character that is perfect. However, make their flaws forgivable, not deal-breakers.

5. But also give your protagonist a glimpse of heroic qualities or relatable ones that the reader can resonate with.

6. Emphasize their inner struggles. Obviously, this is where the transformation might occur. What keeps your protagonist up at night? What will cause them to change? Any character needs a problem or a challenge that will drive the story.

7. Draw upon your own experience when developing your character. The best way to get your message across is if you believe you are the character.

8. Always keep your transformational arc in mind when writing. Try not to deviate.

9. Use sensory language: show the reader how your character is reacting, don't tell.

10. Research. Even if you're writing comes from experience, imagination can only take you so far. Talk to others, use their experience as well.

Establishing a Plot

Characters set in motion evoke a strong interest in any piece of fiction or nonfiction. We empathize with them, but if the plot is static, readers might actually become frustrated. We all need conflict to see a change. We need plot twists, heartwarming and thrilling turning points, and an action sequence that will keep us turning the pages.

One way to keep the reader engaged is by developing the conflict early on in the story and allowing it to develop around the needs of the protagonist to evolve. This, of course, will allow you, as the writer, to focus on the character's development, how the conflict is affecting the said character, and how they will be pushed to mature and grow. Correlating the plot/conflict with the character's maturity and growth doesn't mean you can't have subplots; as long as the other storylines and subplots lead to the final resolution, then it will still keep the reader engaged.

You need to be able to follow the basic story arc and plan ahead so everything will be clear for you before you start writing. It should be able to take on the following timeline, and you can even use this as an outline for your transformational story arc.

Transformational Story Arc Outline

1. The character first faces an inciting incident.	
2. Then a call to action.	
3. A defining moment.	
4. They face their first turning point.	
5. An awakening occurs, and this is when the action starts rising.	
6. They are pushed to their breaking point.	
7. We reach a peak of enlightenment, and this is the climax of the story.	
8. There's a period of grace, and then the falling action occurs.	

9. Let's say they face another tragedy or life-altering experience, like a death.	
10. They face a second turning point.	
11. As the action descends, another transformational moment happens.	
12. Which then leads to the resolution.	

Transformational Themes

A theme is basically what you, as the writer, believe in. It encompasses your vision, your passion, and values. It's your job to answer universal questions through discovery and exploring these questions and the feelings arising with them. The theme can drive your story and make it tangible. This can happen through the action of the protagonist. Themes can revolve around the following:

- **Coming of age:** It's one of the most classical forms of transformational storytelling and the most effective. It will truly show how a character has grown and matured into someone capable of handling challenges.

- **Forgiveness:** Forgiving someone can be one of the hardest things many people have to do. But forgiving yourself trumps that. Stories about forgiveness following a tragedy can help readers define who they are and accept the fate of any situation as well as involved people as well.

- **Letting go:** We walk around with so much shame, guilt, anger, revenge, or even self-esteem issues that often feel like a heavy burden on our shoulders. Finding inner peace and maturing can only happen when we let go.

- **Overcoming fear:** Fear tends to control our life decisions most of our lives. Overcoming it doesn't mean you just face it head-on, it's often more subtle than that. Writing about overcoming fear will allow the reader to take a step back and examine their life choices as well as look at a situation logically.

Developing a Poetic Mindset

Over time, our skills develop. And as much as you feel grateful for the knowledge you have, there are times when you need to find new, creative ways to express what you really want to say. Poetry has often been considered the gateway into writing because so many new writers attempt to start their craft by trying to capture simple expressions and thoughts and display them into poetry.

Developing a poetic mindset, even if you're not writing poems at the moment, can drastically shape your words and thoughts in whatever you write. Sometimes, writing other forms can impact your current style and the quality of your work. You don't even need to be a professional poet, but practicing that skill to enhance the quality of another skill means that you're honing more skills as an artist. Think of it this way; some film actors go back to their roots by performing in small theater shows to sharpen their skills and prepare for their next role. You can do the same by writing poetry in order to develop your other forms of writing and enhance your style.

When you practice the use of vivid imagery and sensory language, it allows your words to stand out completely. Creating rhythm also helps your sentences run smoothly on paper, thus becoming easier to read and comprehend.

Another beneficial aspect of writing poetry is that it allows you to use concise words and statements to make a simple sentence hold a loud message. This gives you the skill of making whatever writing piece you write later brief and straightforward, which will allow your reader to digest your words easily.

All writers want to be heard loud and clear and get their message across. Developing a poetic mindset will enhance your style and quality of work. Consider these exercises below to achieve this mindset.

Try Experimental Methods

Experimental poetry like Blackout Poetry or Erasure poetry is known to increase your creativity because you manipulate and existing piece of text by allowing you to challenge the established language and revive your own point of view. All you have to do is grab a newspaper article or a page from an old book, and with a sharpie, blackout any words you don't want and leave the ones that you do. The revealed words have created a poem about your own vision. (Napoleon, 2018)

Use Dreams to Explore Symbols

Leave a dream journal next to your bed, and anytime you dream of something significant, get up and write about it immediately. You can analyze its elements later or even look up its symbols. Use these elements and symbols in writing your poems or any piece of writing. By doing so, you'll realize that your vision is becoming clear and you have used your inner world, your subconscious in your writing in the outside world.

Writing is a craft that is best developed when you explore other options. At the end of the day, your newly-learned skills spill into your target writing piece, in this case, it's transformational writing. You'll eventually be equipped enough to write a book or any writing piece that is believable, showing your experience, healing and transformational, and interesting and well-written.

CHAPTER 6

Optimizing your Writing

Transformational writing is something that can sometimes feel like you are writing a thesis to your life. And in a way, it is! It is, after all, the application of energy and intention to move the direction of your actions in order to reach your desires and goals. And just like it is imperative to edit any important piece of writing, this too applies to your Law of Attraction statements and records.

The way it works when it comes to the Law of Attraction is that you are not merely 'editing' your expressions of desires, goals, and affirmations, you are optimizing their value and meaning. The road to your destiny is paved with manifestations that are consistently and continuously being 'edited' and updated.

This is why writing is such a pivotal and effective tool for applying the Law of Attraction to your life. By writing, you are able to go back to your records and affirmations and alter them accordingly so that they can be manifested to the best of your ability, giving you the results you desire. So what is it that you need to do in order to effectively edit your transformational writing, to have it work in a way that is conducive to your circumstances? We're going to cover these tools so that you can become a professional at upgrading the manifestation of your desires consistently.

Refining your desires

What is achievable by the process of editing is that you get to refine the purpose and goal of your desires. By doing this, you allow yourself to narrow in on what really matters, or at the very least, prioritize, organize, and filter.

The Value of Clarity

It's a good idea to get yourself another notebook, or several, that serve the purpose of recording your edited version of desires, gratitude, and affirmations. This is purely for organizational purposes, and it will make the process of referring back to the work, comparing notes and upgrading much easier. You also have the option of getting a notebook that is divided into sections if you find this is more convenient for you. Having a new notebook will give you a feeling of renewal. A fresh page offers a fresh look at the confessions and expressions that you have already revealed in your writing.

You may even want to consider taking it a step further and categorizing your desires in different areas in your life. Have a section or notebook devoted to:

-Relationship Goals: How you would like to be treated, what kind of communication you need to have, and the things that cannot be present, as well as the characteristics that you know, will help you in your journey.

-Financial Goals: What you need to do and have in order to have a secure and comfortable life. This will also coincide with the kinds of experiences and possessions you feel you need to have in order to fulfill your desires and goals in life.

-Lifestyle Goals: Health, diet, activities. A healthy body leads to a healthy mind; it really is as simple as that. So find the right kind of diet that you can implement daily, for the rest of your life comfortably- without it having to feel like torture! See what you have tried initially has been fruitful in terms of having you feel better about your health and your body in general.

-Career Goals: What is your passion? What are you good at? What may be your hidden skills? What can you do to excel in your professional life? Discover the things that you've wanted to do all your life and see if you may have a knack for it. Understand how your current job makes you feel and see how it affects your overall mood and the way you treat others- and yourself! Your profession needs to bring out the best in you, and in those around you.

-Bucket List: Things you feel the need to see or do before you die, and why you feel they are so necessary. Separate between the ones you would like to experience out of curiosity, the ones you feel would conquer your fears, and the ones that have sentimental value.

All these achievements lead to a sense of accomplishment within you. They will build on your self-esteem, your knowledge of the world, and your perspective on pretty much everything. You will have a deeper understanding of what it is that you need to attract into your life to give you a sense of security. Making a record of them all reminds you of all of the wonderful things you have done, are doing, and will do at some point in the future. Going a step further and clarifying your goals and desires by spreading them out into different sections will help by miles in being able to put the manifestation into action.

The Importance of Drafting

It would be foolish to assume that we are bound to get things right the very first time we try them. That's not to say that it isn't possible, but in regards to transformational writing for the application of the Law of Attraction into your life in a meaningful and genuine way, then it would be wise to come to terms with the fact that this will take work.

Regardless of whether you are new to the Law of Attraction or have been at it for a long time, it's always necessary to redraft your desires, goals, and methods until you get it absolutely right. Our circumstances in life are ever-changing, and as a result, so are our opinions, perspectives, and our experiences.

When starting off with transformational writing, we'll call the very first attempt Draft A. In this version, just write. Give yourself the freedom to express yourself and let go of anything you may have been stifling within yourself. Whether it be a secret, something from your past or present that you are ashamed of, or a multitude of things that we, as humans, tend to hide from the world around us. While it is encouraged that you try to categorize your writing as much as you can, if you feel you are unable to do this initially, then just write whatever comes to mind at any given time. This is just so the release occurs. Once you feel that you've told your truth, it's important that you try your best to follow the steps and guidance provided in previous chapters so that we are able to get the most out of our writing.

It is Draft B that will lead you to a better understanding of yourself and get you started on your path of releasing energy in order to live by the Law of Attraction. By reading over Draft A, it allows you to look at your life as though you are an outsider looking in, observing the sequence of events, your behavior, and the effects that circumstances and people have on you. By the time you get through the process initially, you will be better equipped to analyze Draft A and weed out the people, goals, and desires that you may no longer need in your life in order to reach higher ground- both in your life as a whole and on a psychological level as well.

One thing that you must remember when it comes to editing your life's work, is that less is more. But only after you actually have the 'more' available! What this means, is that in order to simplify your life and understand your true purpose and reach a place where you can see and achieve the desires that are meant to elevate you as a person- you first have to let it all out. It has to be complex in order to be simplified. This is why the clutter is just as important as the clean-up. Draft A has no filter, while Draft B is the refined, filtered version that paints a clear picture of what your path should look like.

Trial & Error to Edit Effectively

What makes transformational writing different from everyday writing is that the goal is to literally *'transform'* the things that we write into reality. This is why editing this work is of such great importance. We need every draft that comes after the first (*if* there is more than one!) to be edited and written with the intention of manifestation into pure action. Whether it be changes in mental activities and perceptions or physical actions that affect the direction in which our lives are moving- the way we put our desires into writing, and ultimately into the world with our vibrations, is of the utmost value. This is where the activity of trial and error comes in to help us edit our work in an effective way.

You already have your scripting journal to help you draw up a hypothetical prediction of how the Law of Attraction will play into manifesting your desire, should you apply certain affirmations or change specific reactions and general behavior in your life.

When you analyze and clarify your writing, this will, in turn, affect the scripting as well- it will be edited as well. And this is a great way to measure and assume how outcomes can differ if small details differ.

Besides experimenting with changes and edits in your scripting, you will also try out the edited versions of your process of manifestation in real life. There is obviously no better way to know how a thought or an action affects the direction of your life, and the reactions it may conjure as well.

A Better Paved Road to your Destiny

When you really take the time to analyze your desires and why you have them, along with what options you have to achieve them, you will feel much more confident about moving forward towards them. By editing your work, you are polishing up the methods by which you think. You are creating shortcuts and even paving new ways that are more refined and prove to be much more effective in ultimately reaching your goal.

When we use the Law of Attraction, we want to put out more than just thoughts and vibrations. We want to put out clear, solid, and specific messages that are unique to you. The clearer and simpler the desires are made, the smoother the ride to your goal will be.

Creating Standards

The best way to move forward with the editing process is to set standards. You need to create a checklist that you will come up with yourself after you have gone over Draft A. By doing so, you will be able to specify what you need and don't need in order to have the right thoughts and actions that will lead you towards achieving your goals in the most natural and stress free manner.

Let's go over a couple of examples to help illustrate how this works:

- For example, in Draft A, you may notice a couple of people that you mention that help in bringing positivity to your life, and many that cause you to falter. There will definitely be one or two people who stand out. So when are editing to write out Draft B of your manifestation plan, you will know that you need to remind yourself to stay away from the negativity and keep the people that encourage you to grow and do better for yourself.

- You realize that on the days where you wake up and meditate, your overall demeanor and mood are much more pleasant and your thoughts are clearer as opposed to the days that you do not. So from this, you know that you have to be sure to meditate every single day in order to prepare your mind for a productive day.

- You discover that buying a new car didn't do much to help you reach your goal and that it was only a material longing that did not contribute to easing the journey towards your goal. By making this realization, you find that sometimes, spending in excess on material things can disturb your energy because you become too focused on money, and this did not contribute to helping you meet the right person and starting a family. So you learn that in Draft B, spending too much time in perfecting your image in front of others does not prove anything whatsoever. So you edit with that in mind- you change parts of your script to eliminate focus on bettering the material things in your life, and you change the desires that will lead you to your goals.

Moderation is Balance

When you edit your writing, be sure to be mindful of the things that you desire. Anything that you desire in excess or that adds something to your life that really isn't necessary, run the risk of taking you off track. Simplicity and moderation are the key factors to achieving anything worthwhile in life. And while they may seem much too basic, both of these concepts require hard work in a society that thrives off of promoting opulence and excessiveness in everything.

- When you think and write about what you want from a relationship, try your best to stay away from focusing too much on appearance and social standing. This may very well hinder you from finding your true soul mate. Think about your characteristics and your personality, your likes and dislikes, your outstanding features, and your faults. Through this assessment, you will be able to come up with what kind of a person you need in your life to balance you out.

- If one of your goals is to have an early retirement so that you can really enjoy life and see what the world has to offer, then edit your thoughts and writing accordingly. I should live a simple life and not overspend so I can save and retire early. I cannot overwork myself. Otherwise, I will burn out. Work hard and plan well for the future. Keep the possibility of emergency spending occurring. Do not set unrealistic goals and desires that push you to the edge of your ability- this will only stress you out, and you will never be able to reach your goal- even if you do retire early, you will be broken inside- and that defeats the whole purpose.

Trigger phrases & Words

There are certain words and phrases that act as triggers for specific thoughts. While we usually associate this with negative experiences, such as trauma and flashback, these can be very effective tools for using the Law of Attraction effectively.

While reading through the first draft of all your notebooks, and especially the affirmation quotes that you have created, pay close attention. Which words have you repeated the most? What do they make you feel? How do you react?

We encourage the process of writing to provide transformation through the Law of Attraction because communication is an extremely powerful tool. And we often overlook the power of self-communication. The reason we brought to light the importance of accessing the subconscious is that, as you write, you will find that certain words and phrases will automatically bring up images and thoughts into your head. The way to take hold of this is to edit your writing and learn about yourself. The words and conversations that trigger emotions in you are very important to acknowledge so that you can use them to your advantage.

As a starting point, you can use affirmative quotes that you've seen before to get you on your way as your practice applying the Law of Attraction. But once you start the writing process, and you come around to edit, you will become more confident, and you will actually *prefer* to write your own motivational and self-affirming phrases. You will be able to access your strengths whenever you desire in order to get a task done, or get through a tough situation, but by having the thought of these words.

USING KEYWORDS FOR THE LAW OF ATTRACTION

We have gone over what affirmation is and how you can use self-affirmative quotes to help you visualize your desires. Within the editing process, you will discover the words that you love the most. The words that make you feel good, confident, and remind you of who you are and why you want to press on to reach your goal. You will find these words within your confessions in your first draft. You will certainly know how to tailor them to affirmative quotes when you are scripting your future, and you will know how to apply them to real-life situations when you are faced with circumstances that test your faith in yourself.

- If you are working a job that you love, but you find that many people bring you down with their attitude towards you and towards the work in general, this could very well affect you in the worst way possible. If your desire is to reach a position at your job where you have more control and are able to turn things around within the work environment, then you need to find the words to motivate you. If through your writing, you have found that all the struggles that you've faced in your life have taught you to rise from the experience, then that could very well be a trigger word for you. So use it!

- 'I will *rise* above the negativity and focus on growing.'

- I will help anyone who is struggling to *rise* above their challenges.'

You'll find that in due time, these are not merely words that you are repeating. You will soon understand the value and effectiveness of keywords that are personal to you. Many that are connected to something from your past, and many that you will decide to make a part of your future-simply because you *chose* these words to create an effect and to release a demeanor, an energy and a feeling of vibration that no one that meets you can deny. You will understand how delivery to yourself and to others makes a world of difference. Once you are able to create a system and criteria for *how* you want to edit and what kind of words you are looking to use, you will see how much more influential each phrase you speak will be on your subconscious, and those around you.

Don't forget your gift!

Here is a **FREE** video training course on how to develop Relentless Optimism

Positive thinking is a state of mind that naturally expects a positive outcome to events. Not all of us were born to be positive thinkers. The good news is that this mindset is a habit that can be developed and enhanced.

The benefits are greater happiness and the increased likelihood that you will be able to achieve whatever goals you create for yourself. Positive thinking knows no limits, while negative thoughts only create limitations.

Click the picture of the DVD box or navigate to the link below to claim your copy now!

https://tinyurl.com/RelentlessOptimism

CONCLUSION

Now that you have read through the book and understand the theory as well the application of the Law of Attraction, you can really go into it with confidence. You are the conductor of your destiny, and only you can bring positivity and success into your world. There's no psychedelic secret written in the stars, and there's no complex formula that you need to decipher using an ancient language! There is only the journey of self-assessment, self- discovery, and self-affirmation.

Key Points of Transformational Writing

As humans, we are a unique and intriguing species. We are complex and intelligent, and we have so many layers to us- a human mind is a wondrous tool that is capable of so much more than we know but is slowly discovering through science, psychology, and the power of the different levels of consciousness.

By reading this book, you can now link and connect the dots between your understanding of the Law of Attraction, how different forms and activities of writing can help you make new and old discoveries about yourself, and how through writing, you can finally take the necessary steps and action to help you bring your desires to life, and one step closer to your ultimate goals in life.

After you're done reading this book, you should have a clear understanding of:

- Understanding what the Law of Attraction is

- The value of language in our everyday life and its role in applying the Law of Attraction

- Information about influential people that live by the Law of Attraction and how they do so

- The operational principles that need to be applied for you to get results consistently

- A look into how science is integrated into the principle of the Law of Attraction

- How thoughts & vibrations are intertwined

- How to rewire your brain in order to have it function on positivity rather than negativity

- The different levels of consciousness and how to access and understand the information you discover through writing and analysis, as well as guidance.

- The categories of thoughts and behavior

- What positive cognition is all about

- The value of self-awareness and self-discipline

- What desires are and how they work- and how to make them work for you

- The Law of Vibrations

- A clear understanding of affirmations and their role in the Law of Attraction

- Using techniques and exercises to manifest your dreams

- How to utilize meditation and hypnosis as tools to delve into your past and your subconscious in order to better understand yourself to solve and overcome any negative aspects in your life

- How to create effective Law of Attraction journals and how they can change your perception as well as clarify your goals and desires

- The process of goal-setting

- How to bring all your knowledge together through writing

- The importance of scripting and productive visualization

- The art of powerful writing and effective editing, and how they curate the steps of your journey towards your goals

Revelations

Once you're done reading this book, you'll discover that every waking moment, every day of your life is filled with revelations. About you, your perception, your hopes, dreams, and desires. Allowing yourself to confidently believe that you really *can* have control over the events that occur in your life will give you a newfound sense of freedom.

The Law of Attraction teaches us about the importance of things our fast-paced lives, and our upbringing may have shut down. The value of acknowledging your instinct and gut feelings are torn apart by insecurities and experiences that make us doubt ourselves.

Once you begin to apply Transformational Writing, along with the exercises mentioned throughout the book, you'll find that you are able to do so much more for you and the people around you just by identifying who you are and what you need to have a fulfilled lifestyle.

There will always be skepticism thrown at theories and methodologies as well as ideologies that are not 100% backed up by scientific proof. But remember that there are many scientific theories that were thought to be illogical and irrelevant that could only be proved after the passage of time when we had the right technology and means to discover the proof. The point being, just because it doesn't have scientific proof or the go-ahead from scientists as legitimate, this doesn't mean it doesn't exist or that it is not credible and effective. Mankind has only advanced through the belief of a few that dared to defy the norms and rules of society in order to elevate our minds.

With the Law of Attraction, your states of consciousness are what hold the keys to developing the art of achieving the means to fulfill your life's goals. There are so many parts of our minds that have not been tapped into, and if we are ever to discover them and their purpose, we have to believe and delve deep. The Law of Attraction allows you to *believe*. Whether it's in a higher being or a higher cause, yourself and others- the possibility and scope of the concept of 'belief' is limitless. And you'll find that, the more you believe, the more you discover, the more you learn.

Using Transformational Writing to embed the Law of Attraction into your life is the greatest tool you will work with. Simply put, expression is everything. This is really no surprise- we have spent all our lives living in fantasy worlds, seeing characters that do not exist in the real world and living their lives through their eyes with every book we have read and loved growing up. Many of these characters stuck with us throughout our lives and we idolized them too. This is your first experience with transformational writing. This is how another person's words changed your perception through fictitious characters. And now, that you have understood the value of the Law of Attraction, it's now your turn to change your life with your own words using real-life tools and applications. From accessing your subconscious, whether it be through introspection, therapy, or hypnosis, to creating your own script for your life and coming up with your own affirmations. You are now the author of your own fantasy where all your dreams can actually become your reality.

THANK YOU…..

We cannot teach gratitude without expressing it ourselves! This book is the fruit of the labor of love. The greatest gratitude goes out to you, for allowing yourself to explore an important concept that will change your life, just as it has with so many others. The Law of Attraction is something that keeps on giving, only if you let it thrive. Thank you to all the influential people that stood in the face of adversity, ridicule, and skepticism and persevered in order to educate us and bring us closer to ourselves. Also, to the many scientists and psychologists that allowed themselves to break free of the walls that say 'no' without looking beyond what is in solid form. Our minds are magical and hold powers that we can no longer take for granted, simply because we now have the tools and the capacity to look beyond what is in plain sight.

WORKS CITED

Bernstein, G. (2014). *Miracles Now: 108 Life-Changing Tools for Less Stress, More Flow, and Finding Your True Purpose.*

Byrne, R. (2006). *The Secret* . Beyond Words Publishing.

Chopra, D. (2019, August). *Ask Deepak*. Retrieved from www.oprah.com: http://www.oprah.com/spirit/how-the-law-of-attraction-works-ask-deepak

Cooper, A. (2007). *Our Ultimate Reality, Life, the Universe and Destiny of Mankind.*

Gallagher, S. (2006). *How the body shapes the mind - An interview with Shaun Gallagher*. Retrieved from Science & Consciousness: http://www.sci-con.org/2006/01/how-the-body-shapes-the-mind-an-interview-with-shaun-gallagher/

Gerke, J. (2010). *Plot Versus Character: A Balanced Approach to Writing Great Fiction.* Writer's Digest Books.

Grierson, B. (2014). *What if Age Is Nothing but a Mind-Set?* Retrieved from The New York Times Magazine: https://www.nytimes.com/2014/10/26/magazine/what-if-age-is-nothing-but-a-mind-set.html?_r=0

Hallbom, K., & Hallbom, T. (n.d.). *Exploring the Neuroscience and Magic Behind Setting Your Intent – And Creating an Optimal Future for Yourself.* Retrieved from https://www.nlpca.com/creating-an-optimal-future-for-yourself.html: https://www.nlpca.com/creating-an-optimal-future-for-yourself.html

Hassabis, D., & Maguire, E. (2009). *Philosophical transactions of the Royal Society of London.* Retrieved from NCBI: https://www.ncbi.nlm.nih.gov/pmc/articles/PMC2666702/

Juhasz, B. J., Yap, M. J., Dicke, J., Taylor, S. C., & Gullick, M. (2011). Tangible words are recognized faster: The grounding of meaning in sensory and perceptual systems. *The Quarterly Journal of Experimental Psychology* , 1683-1691.

Lacey, S., Stilla, R., & Sathian, K. (2012). Metaphorically feeling: Comprehending textural metaphors activates somatosensory cortex. *Brain and Language*, 416-421.

Marks, D. (2006). *Inside Story: The Power of the Transformational Arc.* Three Mountain Press.

Napoleon, N. (2018). *Creativity Exercises: 3 Ways to Awaken Your Mind to Poetic Thinking*. Retrieved from Writer's Digest: https://www.writersdigest.com/editor-blogs/poetic-asides/advice/ways-awaken-your-mind-poetry-poetic-thinking

Newberg, A., & Waldmen, M. R. (2012). *Words Can Change Your Brain* . New York : Penguin Group .

Proctor, B. (n.d.). *The Law of Vibration as Explained by Bob Proctor.* Retrieved from The Wisdom Post: http://www.thewisdompost.com/motivational-speakers/bob-proctor/law-vibration-explained-bob-proctor/1761

Raab, D. (2017). *Writing for Bliss: A Seven-Step Plan for Telling Your Story and Transforming Your Life.* Loving Healing Press.

Raz, A., Kirsch, I., Pollard, J., & Nitkin-Kaner, Y. (2005). Suggestion Reduces the Stroop Effect. *Psychological Science* .

Wheeler, J., & Folger, T. (2002). *Does the Universe Exist if We're Not Looking?* Retrieved from Discover Magazine: http://discovermagazine.com/2002/jun/featuniverse

Yonsei Medical Journal. (2007). Retrieved from NCBI: https://www.ncbi.nlm.nih.gov/pmc/articles/PMC2628098/